Laurie, Tom
With best wishes

Francis Wilson.

DINOSAURS, DIAMONDS AND DEMOCRACY

October 2009.

DINOSAURS, DIAMONDS AND DEMOCRACY

A short, short history of South Africa

FRANCIS WILSON

UMUZI

Published by Umuzi 2009
PO Box 6810, Roggebaai 8012, South Africa,
an imprint of Random House Struik (Pty) Ltd
Company Reg No 1966/003153/07
80 McKenzie Street, Cape Town 8001, South Africa
PO Box 1144, Cape Town 8000, South Africa
umuzi@randomstruik.co.za
www.umuzi-randomhouse.co.za

First edition, first printing 2009
1 3 5 7 9 8 6 4 2

ISBN 978-1-4152-0086-5

Cover design by mr design
Text design by William Dicey
Set in Sabon and Meta
Printed and bound by Times Offset (M)
Sdn Bhd, Malaysia

TABLE OF CONTENTS

For my colleagues and friends in the universities of South Africa from whom, over many years, I have learnt so much – not least during the course of writing this book.

&

In memory of Stephen Bantu Biko – who loved history, debated it passionately and encouraged me to write more about it.

INTRODUCTION

A HISTORY OF SOUTH AFRICA IN 18 000 WORDS? It is perhaps foolish to try to encapsulate in so short a book a history which stretches back to the beginning of life itself. A brief text can, however, provide an illuminating overview for the visitor to South Africa, as well as for those South Africans without the time or means to read more deeply. It can also serve as a stimulus for those who wish to study further, using one or more of the many excellent single- or multi-volume histories of the country.

To many people South Africa is known chiefly for its beautiful landscapes, its wild animals, its gold mines and for the oppression of apartheid. But there is far more to the country than that. The Cradle of Humankind, a World Heritage Site outside Johannesburg, bears testimony to the importance of South Africa in the evolution of human beings. The subsequent immigration of people over the past 2 000 years created a melting pot in which the central theme, as has been argued in *The Oxford History of South Africa*, is 'interaction between peoples of diverse origins, languages, technologies, ideologies and social systems meeting on South African soil'. The discovery of all kinds of minerals over the past century and more has turned the country into the jewellery box of the world. And the political transition, led by Nelson Mandela, from a racist state to a modern democracy has aroused admiration around the globe: an admiration somewhat tempered, though, by current concerns about the country's future.

Undoubtedly, there will be critics of such a concise work, especially when the subject is as unresolved and controversial as the history of South Africa. Were the Dutch and the English who came to South Africa in the 17th and 19th centuries 'settlers' or 'invaders'? What of the Bantu-speaking iron and pottery workers from the north, who crossed the Limpopo River into the land of the San and the Khoe between 2 000 and 1 500 years ago? When – and from where – did the Khoe, pastoral people, acquire their sheep and cattle? Even the palaeontological history, going back hundreds of thousands of years, has been evolving rapidly in recent decades and many crucial questions are far from settled. In our own day, there are very different perspectives on the relations between black and white and on the role of different political groups within the liberation movement.

It is not possible to include in a book of this nature enough to satisfy all of its readers. If it does no more than whet the appetites of the curious, so that they catch a glimpse of just how fascinating the history of South Africa is, no matter how recent, nor how far back one goes, then it will have done its job. But if it can also help to facilitate, in some small way, further debate about controversial aspects of the past, then it will indeed have achieved all that can be hoped for. For those who wish to read more, a list of further reading has been prepared online at www.umuzi-randomhouse.co.za, where detailed endnotes on sources may also be found. Opportunity is also provided there for readers to write their own blogs – comments, corrections, criticisms or questions, all of which will add to the debate as we seek to forge a common history for all South Africans.

1
ONCE UPON A TIME ...

South Africa can lay claim to being the cradle of life. In the
Barberton Mountains east of Johannesburg ancient greenstone
rocks, which formed part of the world's first continent, known
as Kaapvaal, preserve the fossilised remains of ancient bacteria
and record the earliest evidence of life 3.5 billion years ago. Other
rocks, formed at various times over many thousands of millions
of years, provide an astonishing record of the development of
life. South Africa, although five times the size of Great Britain,
and more than twice the size of France, comprises only 4% of the
African continent. Yet, within these borders is packed a wealth of
both pre-human and human history.

A view of the Barberton Mountains with granite rocks
in the foreground.

The Vredefort Dome, at the centre of the original crater, as seen from space.

2.02 billion years ago a huge asteroid hit the ground near the site where Vredefort stands today. In the process it created a crater some 250 km in diameter. South Africa's major gold mines all lie within this area.

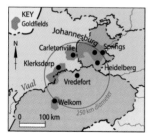

LET'S START AT THE SITE OF THE SMALL TOWN OF Vredefort, 120 km south-west of Johannesburg. Here, around 2.02 billion years ago, an enormous asteroid, somewhat larger than Cape Town's Table Mountain, came hurtling in from space at approximately 100 times the speed of sound and hit the ground with a force estimated to have been 7 or 8 billion times greater than that of the atomic bomb which destroyed Hiroshima in 1945. The asteroid turned the earth inside out as the pressure of its impact caused soil and rock to rebound from 20 km below the surface. The rock and soil formed a dome in the centre of the crater, which itself settled into a relatively shallow basin with a diameter of 250 to 300 km. Gold-rich layers of rock known as reefs sagged downward around the edges of the crater, tilting them towards the focal point of the impact, after which they were quickly covered by falling rock, debris and dust. These gold deposits were thus protected from erosion, which would otherwise have washed them away over time. The arc of gold mines which curves out from either side of Johannesburg, through the West Rand and Klerksdorp, to Welkom in the Free State traces the outer circle (known as the Witwatersrand) of the original crater. The Vredefort explosion was caused by the largest and first known asteroid to have hit the earth. Had it happened many million years later, it would have caused untold destruction to life; however, only bacteria existed at the time. Not until some 550 million years ago did life begin to evolve into more complex forms.

Since the Vredefort explosion, five major extinction

events have occurred; the worst of these, around 251 million years ago, destroyed about 96% of all then existing species and changed the course of the evolution of life dramatically. The best land-based record of this event is preserved in the dry Karoo, where the fossilised remains of the creatures that lived there before and after this global catastrophe are embedded in rock.

Two-thirds of the surface area of South Africa is covered by rocks of the Karoo Supergroup. These rocks contain an unsurpassed record of the development of life on land over the 100-million-year period between 280 and 180 million years ago, a period that witnessed the evolutionary origin and appearance of the first mammals, tortoises and dinosaurs. South Africa is renowned for having the most complete fossil set of therapsids, an extinct group of animals that record

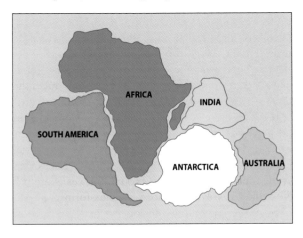

About 180 million years ago Gondwana, the great southern supercontinent, began to split up. India drifted slowly north, crashing into Asia and creating the Himalaya Mountains in the process.

The Drakensberg. South Africa's major mountain range runs north–south down most of the eastern side of the country. It rises to a height of 3 482 metres, is often capped with snow in winter, and is home to many of the finest San paintings.

A fossilised skeleton of the therapsid *Trirachodon*. In the Karoo there are many fossils, which together provide an un-broken record of 100 million years during which mammals evolved from reptile-like ancestors.

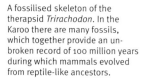

the evolutionary transition between early reptile-like forms and mammals.

Also in the Karoo rocks, from the foothills of the Drakensberg (which means 'Dragon Mountain'), are fossils of some of the oldest known dinosaurs. These include the oldest dinosaur eggs (200 million years old), which contain beautifully preserved embryos – less than 10 cm long – of the dinosaur *Massospondylus*, as well as the oldest sauropods (the group to which the largest long-necked dinosaurs belong). There is also a younger dinosaur from the Eastern Cape named with an isiXhosa click: *Nqwebasaurus*. Dinosaurs were present throughout the world 180 million years ago and dominated the landscape until they succumbed to an extinction event 65 million years ago. The vertebrate survivors, which included small nocturnal mammals, went on to populate the globe.

An imaginative drawing of *Nqwebasaurus*, a dinosaur whose fossilised bones were discovered in the eastern Cape in 1996. It is estimated to be about 135 million years old.

Twenty million years ago saw a radiation of the anthropoid primates that ultimately gave rise to hominids such as orang-utans, gorillas, chimpanzees and humans. These early hominids shared an African landscape dominated by vast herds of different grazing animals, from antelope to zebra, which were hunted by predators such as hyena, leopard and lion.

A tiny embryo of the dinosaur *Massospondylus* found inside a fossilised egg. It was discovered in the eastern Free State and is estimated to be almost 200 million years old.

WORLD HERITAGE SITES

South Africa contains eight World Heritage Sites as proclaimed by UNESCO (see the map on p. 121):

- Fossil hominid sites of Sterkfontein, Swartkrans, Kromdraai, and environs (The Cradle of Humankind)
- iSimangaliso (St Lucia) Wetland Park
- Robben Island
- uKhahlamba-Drakensberg Park
- The Mapungubwe Cultural Landscape
- The Cape Floral Region
- The Vredefort Dome
- The Richtersveld Cultural and Botanical Landscape

Africa's savannah grassland was ideally suited for the evolution of predators such as lions.

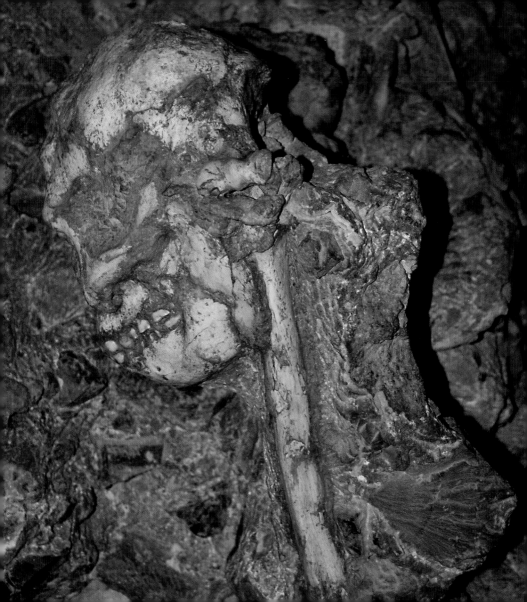

2
THE GREAT BREAKTHROUGH

The transition from pre-human to human history took place in Africa. A series of fossil discoveries provides clear evidence that *Homo sapiens* emerged in Africa about 200 000 years ago, whilst recent analysis of a skull found in South Africa helps to confirm current thinking that modern humans spread out of Africa to occupy the rest of the world relatively recently – about 50 to 60 000 years ago. Further evidence shows how human beings gradually acquired the skills that have helped them become the dominant species on earth. Of these, the most important have been the capacity to communicate through complex language and to think symbolically.

Australopithecus at Sterkfontein. This photograph from the *South African Journal of Science* shows the skull and another bone of one of the most complete skeletons yet discovered of an ancient hominid. Estimated to be at least 3 million years old, 'Little Foot' joins the Taung child, Mrs Ples and others in the mounting evidence of the importance of South Africa in the long process of human evolution.

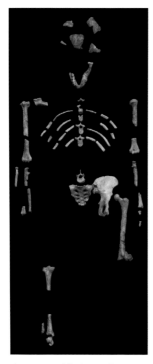

Lucy, a surprisingly complete skeleton of a female *Australopithecus afarensis*, was discovered in Ethiopia in 1974.

A skull of an adult *Australopithecus africanus* was found at Sterkfontein in 1947. The area is today known as the Cradle of Humankind. The skull became known as Mrs Ples.

THE DISCOVERY, IN 1925, OF A REMARKABLY COMplete fossil skull from Taung, west of Kimberley in the Northern Cape, radically changed our understanding of human origins. This skull of a child, described as *Australopithecus africanus* ('southern ape from Africa'), was considered to be the 'missing link' between apes and humans. Subsequent discoveries of other hominids in the Sterkfontein area near Johannesburg – now known as the Cradle of Humankind – led to the recognition that humanity had its origins in southern Africa. Discoveries being made on an ongoing basis at various sites in South Africa corroborate this theory.

A particularly exciting discovery was made in 1947 at Sterkfontein when the skull of an adult *Australopithecus africanus* was found. She is known as 'Mrs Ples'. Thirty years later, a 3.2-million-year-old skeleton of a

Many of the bones in the dolomite caves in the Cradle of Humankind are believed to have come from carcasses dragged there by leopards to hide them from scavengers.

Kromdraai, at the Cradle of Humankind, where stone tools estimated to be 1 million years old have been found.

female *Australopithecus afarensis* was found in Ethiopia. She is known as 'Lucy', after the Beatles' song which was playing in the palaeoanthropologists' camp the night after the discovery. In the 1990s an even more complete fossilised skeleton informally known as 'Little Foot' was discovered at Sterkfontein. This remarkable specimen, still in the process of being excavated, has a foot with a slightly divergent big toe, indicating Little Foot's position between apes and humans. Further hominids continue to be discovered in the same area.

Research on the breakage patterns on fossil bones associated with the hominids in the Cradle of Humankind shows that the reason many of these fossils are preserved in caves in the Sterkfontein Valley is because they were carried there and eaten by carnivores such

The crowned eagle (*Stephanoaetus coronatus*) is powerful enough to carry away a monkey or a small human, as seems – from the scratches on its skull – to have happened to the Taung child about 2.2 million years ago.

The Taung child (right), found near Kimberley in 1925, was scientifically named *Australopithecus*, meaning 'southern ape', and immediately recognised as a possible link in the chain of human evolution.

as leopards. Talon marks and indentations on the skull of the Taung child indicate that it was the victim of an eagle attack, as happens periodically to young children even today.

Along the road to becoming human, our ancestors learnt two crucial techniques: the manufacture of tools and the use of fire. It is not yet clear whether any of the australopithecines made stone tools, but what is certain is that the genus which followed them, labelled *Homo* (and distinguished from *Paranthropus* or *Australopithecus* primarily by their larger brain) were definitely tool-makers.

Argument continues as to whether or not *Homo habilis* mastered language, but all are agreed that *Homo erectus*, who emerged approximately 2 million years ago, can be regarded as the first clearly identifiable

LANGUAGE

Tools were important, control of fire was important, development of the brain was vital, but none of these alone accounted for human beings as we know them today. The fundamental breakthrough in human development was the acquisition of language. Anybody who has heard a disparate collection of birds warning of the danger of a snake nearby, or seen a sentinel baboon grunt or gesticulate high up on a prominent rock, will know that animals can communicate about danger or, like bees, about the source of food. But more complex communication and cooperation require symbolic thinking and language.

Human beings, whichever of the world's 5 000 or more languages they are speaking, have a large vocabulary and use a wide range of concepts. Parts of these vocabularies, like the 350 or more different isiXhosa or isiZulu words to describe the colour patterns on Nguni cattle, may be specific to a particular culture, but they are no less sophisticated than, say, the names of atomic particles used in modern physics. In contrast, our nearest evolutionary relatives, chimpanzees, cannot learn to use more than about 400 words: a vocabulary that can be mastered by a three-year-old child. An average adult can master at least 4 000 words,

A cleaver (top) and hand-axe from the Early Stone Age. The Early Stone Age lasted for over 2 million years, from 2.6 million to 250 000 years ago; the Middle Stone Age for some 200 000 years, from 250 000 to 40 000 years ago; and the Late Stone Age from 40 000 years ago until relatively recently.

Two of Leigh Voigt's paintings of Nguni cattle. Inala (top), meaning 'abundance', with red or brown spots all over its body and 'horns like a wide-brimmed hat'; and Ilunga (bottom), with the strong black-and-white markings of a fiscal shrike.

with a vocabulary of 100 000 not unusual. Current thinking is that more complex human language and symbolic thinking began to emerge somewhere between 150 000 and 50 000 years ago. By this time *Homo sapiens*, maker of tools, controller of fire and effective communicator was, as we have seen, beginning to move out of Africa into Asia and Europe to inhabit virtually the whole planet.

human ancestor. This was the hominid who not only made and used stone hand-axes, but also, a million years ago, first used fire. The earliest evidence for the controlled use of fire is to be found at Swartkrans Cave in the Cradle of Humankind.

Only between 200 000 and 100 000 years ago do we begin to find clear evidence of the emergence of modern humans: *Homo sapiens*. The oldest reliably dated specimen from 195 000 years ago was found in Kenya. In South Africa, the oldest anatomically modern humans were found at Klasies River mouth west of Port Elizabeth – dating from around 100 000 years ago; while a human skull, found just south of Swaziland, dates back 75 000 years. A much younger skull, also from the Eastern Cape, near the small dorp (village) of Hofmeyr, was found to be 36 000 years old and demonstrates that only after human beings spread out of Africa 50 000 years ago did modern geographic variability emerge.

GLOBAL MELTING-POT

Sarah Tishkoff and her colleagues have recently published research which shows inter alia that the population known to genetic scientists as 'Cape Mixed Ancestry' and living mainly in the Western Cape (and once classified 'Coloured' under apartheid's Population Registration Act) shows the highest levels of intercontinental admixture of any population in the world. The genetic evidence shows that 25% of their ancestry can be traced to southern African Khoesan, 20% to India, 19% to the Niger–Kordofanian language group, which is spoken across a broad region of Africa, and 19% to Europe. A further 8% of their ancestry can be traced to east Asia (which is surprisingly low). Clearly the Cape has been one of the world's great meeting grounds since human beings first began to leave Africa some 50 000 years ago.

Sarah Tishkoff et al., 'The Genetic Structure and History of Africans and African Americans', Sciencexpress, *30.04.2009*

3
GATHERERS, FISHERS & HUNTERS

After language, the next great breakthrough in human evolution was the discovery, in the relatively recent past, of how to domesticate both plants and animals for purposes of farming. For hundreds of thousands of years before that, human beings had to gather food wherever they could find it. There is abundant evidence in South Africa, from archaeological sites all over the country (some going back 100 000 years or more) of what people ate. And much more than that: over time, human beings learnt to make ornaments; to paint; to dance; to think about the world around them. Early evidence of all these activities is to be found in South Africa and it is possible to piece together a good idea of the sorts of lives people were living here in the millennia before settled agriculture.

Shellfish on the rocks between high and low tide, as seen in this photograph by Neil Rusch, have for 100 000 years or more been a favourite food of human beings.

DURING THE 100 000 YEARS AND MORE BEFORE farming began, human beings had to gather their food where they could: berries, roots and the flesh of such edible animals or insects as they could catch. There was, of course, another crucial source of food – the sea. South Africa, with ocean on three sides, has 3 000 km of coastline. With the cold Benguela current flowing north from the Antarctic and mingling, near Cape Town, with the warm Agulhas current flowing down the east coast, there is a wide variety of seafood in the region. The zone along the shore, between high and low tide, was naturally the best place to gather seafood, a vital source of protein for the developing brain of early humans – shellfish, unlike four-legged game, cannot run away! Archaeologists working through hundreds of middens (ancient rubbish dumps) along

Stone fish traps at Stilbaai.

the South African coast are finding a rich source of dietary information going back 100 000 years. Coastal landscapes are increasingly being seen as the areas where humans are likely to have first evolved – with the Cape being a forerunner.

Whilst scientists are not yet sure at what exact stage in human evolution tools – some of which are 2.6 million years old – were first developed, recent evidence from the Wonderwerk ('Miracle') Cave near Kuruman in the heart of South Africa, suggests that the making of the small tools of the Middle Stone Age 250 000 years ago may have coincided with the emergence of *Homo sapiens*. Over time, human beings became steadily more adept at fashioning the tools they needed to feed themselves. Somewhere between 40 000 and 25 000 years ago, a gradually more sophisticated use of even smaller tools and artefacts ushered in the Late Stone Age. Ranging from meat cleavers to arrowheads, the diversity of stone tools includes a round stone with a hole through the middle. Found at various places in southern Africa, these are thought to have been used as a weight (held fast with a wooden wedge) at the lower end of a stick to facilitate digging down for edible roots or water. Another example – although the dates are uncertain – are the well-preserved stone-wall fish traps at Stilbaai and elsewhere in the Western Cape.

Perhaps the most astonishing example of the skills acquired by our ancestors to feed themselves was their capacity to track and hunt game. It is a skill which has not entirely died out. A traveller in the Kalahari

San armed for hunting.

Using a digging stick weighted with a stone.

A San hunter with bow and arrow.

A patterned ochre fragment (below right) which, with the pierced shells below, was uncovered in Blombos Cave on the southern coast east of Cape Town in 1992.

These pierced shells (possibly used as ornaments) are estimated to be at least 75 000 years old. Together with the ochre fragment, they provide evidence of both art and symbolic thinking by human beings far earlier than was previously thought.

desert in the mid-20th century, after explaining the San capacity to read marks in the sand left by animals, birds and insects, described how he was laughed at by one of them for not even being able to recognise a footprint belonging to his own cook! The San showed that it was not only a matter of reading tracks, deciphering broken twigs or bent grass, or of shooting poisoned arrows with deadly accuracy. They also had the capacity to run alongside an animal until it could run no further.

Evidence that life for early humans entailed more than just hunting for food is provided by discoveries of decorated artefacts and rock and cave paintings in many countries. In a coastal cave east of Cape Town, an exciting find of pierced shells and a patterned ochre fragment enabled archaeologists to push back the earliest known instance of art and jewellery to some 77 000 years ago. Fragments of decorated ostrich shell, including a piece from the rim of a water flask, was a further remarkable discovery. Pigment smeared inside shells has enabled scientists to conclude with reasonable

A San painting on a rock in the Cederberg.

certainty that people in the western Cape have been making paint for the last 10 000 years, at least.

A more recent find, but no less striking, is the clear painting of human figures on a cave wall on the Cape west coast at Steenbokfontein (near Lambert's Bay) painted about 3 500 years ago. The wealth of rock paintings in southern Africa – from the Cape to the Zambezi River there are an estimated 30 000 sites – conveys invaluable information about human history, a hunter–gatherer past that lasted, for some groups of people, for millennia and well into the 19th century.

In the late 19th century a small group of San – modern-day hunters and gatherers – from the northern Cape was released from prison in Cape Town (where they had been incarcerated for stock-theft) to work with a German-born linguist, Wilhelm Bleek, who began developing an orthography of this San language. His sister-in-law, Lucy Lloyd, continued for many years after his death. Conveying in written

This striking painting shows males, who were the hunters of large game, carrying arrows with bone points.

//kabbo.

!kweiten ta //ken came from the Katkop Mountains north of Calvinia.

THE RAIN THAT IS MALE

The rain that is male is an angry rain.
It brings with it lightning loud like our fear.
It brings water storming, making smoke out
    of dust
And we, we beat our navels with our rigid fists.

We, we press a hand, flat to the navel.
We snap our fingers at the angry, male rain.
And we stand outside in the force of the water,
We stand out in the open, close to its thunder,

We snap our fingers and chant while it falls:
'Rain, be gone quickly! Fall but be gone!
Rain, turn away! Turn back from this place!
Rain, take your anger, be gone from our place!'

For we want the other, the rain that is female,
The one that falls softly, soaking into the ground,
The one we can welcome, feeding the plains
So bushes sprout green, springbok come
    galloping.

Version from the /xam by Stephen Watson,
Return of the Moon, *Cape Town, 1991*

form the various clicks used in speaking by these men was something of a challenge. The San individuals – //kabbo, /han=kass'o, !kweiten ta //ken and others – taught Bleek and Lloyd their language. The stories of the /xam, written down in nearly 13 000 pages of interviews, constitute the most complete record of the reality of a hunter–gatherer community that exists anywhere in the world: a world in which the wind, sand and stars were as real and close as other humans; a world permeated by music, poetry and – as always in this dry land – thoughts about water.

4
AGE OF IRON: c.200–c.1500

Farming did not begin in South Africa. About 2000 years ago the herding of sheep and cattle reached South Africa, followed 300 years later by Bantu-speaking farmers. These newcomers brought other techniques too, including the ability to make pottery and to smelt iron and copper. Later, they developed within South Africa the skills to work gold and to build with stone. Trading also began to develop as people exchanged goods. All this made possible the emergence of larger, more complex political systems, such as the Mapungubwe state in Limpopo, where, by the 13th century, there were some 5000 inhabitants in the capital alone. Those who arrived from further north did not, of course, remain isolated from those who were already here. Early evidence of sheep and cattle herding in the western Cape, and of the absorption into the most southern Bantu language (isiXhosa) of indigenous clicks such as those used by the San, is testimony to a long history of interaction.

This clay head, one of seven found broken near Lydenberg in Mpumalanga, dates from the Early Iron Age in the first millennium, somewhere between 200 A.D. and 900 A.D.

AFTER AGRICULTURE, NOTABLY FARMING WITH sheep, goats and some grain, developed on the Fertile Crescent – hills running up the eastern Mediterranean coast and curving east, round the sources of the Tigris and Euphrates rivers – the cultivation of grain and domestication of animals emerged independently in a number of different parts of the world. Southern Africa, however, was not one of them. Sorghum and millet were first domesticated in the Sahel and cattle possibly in north Africa. Whilst there is some evidence of pottery and sheep farming in the arid northern Cape – where neither cattle nor crops could survive – a little more than 2000 years ago, the first large influx of iron-using farmers seems to have been about 300 to 400 years later. People speaking Bantu languages that included an ancestral form of Shona, the language which is the mother tongue of three-quarters of to-day's Zimbabweans, brought with them a good deal of

A Khoe man on his riding ox accompanied by a San on foot (detail from a painting by Thomas Baines, 1863).

A Khoe woman (right), in a sketch by Samuel Daniell.

new knowledge, not only in terms of agriculture, but also in terms of making pottery and smelting metal. The evidence from their settlements – south of the Limpopo River somewhere between 350 and 450 A.D. – provides a tantalising insight into a world of people whose economy was clearly no longer one of hunting and gathering only. The new arrivals brought with them millet and sorghum, and they herded sheep, cattle and possibly goats.

Several hundred years before these immigrants arrived from the north, there was interaction between San hunters and Khoe pastoralists, a group whose early history is still uncertain. Were they originally San who acquired from the north sheep, and later cattle, and who thus, enjoying a better, more regular diet, grew somewhat taller? Or did they themselves migrate from the north, bringing domestic animals with them? Certainly there was intermarriage and absorption all round.

Archaeological evidence of the Early Iron Age is to be found throughout the first millennium (c. 300–c. 1300) in the frost-free Bushveld of the north-eastern part of South Africa, which falls in the country's summer-rainfall regions.

A wide range of eastern and southern African Early Iron Age pottery – called the Chifumbaze complex – is stylistically very similar. One of these sites in particular, which is situated near Lydenburg in Mpumalanga (to the east of Johannesburg) and dates back to the 6th century, combines pottery and a number of remarkable clay heads with cattle enclosure, huts and fragments of

A clay man from Schroda.

A clay elephant from Schroda, made about 1700 years ago.

Although discovered at Mapungubwe in the 1930s, the golden rhinoceros, a symbol of authority dating from the 13th century, was hidden from the public during the apartheid period as its existence contradicted official myths then current about Bantu-speaking people.

iron, copper and ivory – and tells us much about life in South Africa 1 500 years ago.

Up until about 900 A.D., Early Iron Age people farmed in relatively small chiefdoms. However, significant changes in political scale began to take place as evidenced in three important settlements which are to be found just south of the Limpopo River. Schroda was established first in about 900 A.D., with a population estimated at between 350 and 500 people. In the second capital, K2, established a century later, about 1 500 people lived together making pottery, smelting copper and using iron. They were also cultivators, growing sorghum, millet and other crops. They spoke an old form of Shona. Two hundred years later, at the beginning of the 13th century, the capital moved a short distance to Mapungubwe, which became the first settlement in southern Africa to boast 5 000 inhabitants. The new capital provides the first evidence of class structure in

The technique of building the dry stone walls of Great Zimbabwe, shown here, was first developed at Mapungubwe, south of the Limpopo River, by people speaking an ancestral Shona.

southern Africa, with the rulers living on top of the hill – where rain-making took place – and the commoners in the valley below. The famous golden rhino, a symbol of authority, comes from the royal cemetery on the top of the hill. It was at Mapungubwe, with its stone walls, where the building techniques used over the next two centuries at Great Zimbabwe were pioneered. Mapungubwe's inhabitants traded ivory and gold with people on the Indian Ocean coast and imported glass beads from India and glazed stoneware from China. This global trade provided the wealth elites used to accumulate greater political power.

Later immigrants – groupings of them each speaking one of several mutually intelligible dialects of ancestral Nguni – moved down the east coast of South

Mapungubwe was established at the beginning of the 13th century. With an estimated population of 5 000 people, it was the first small town in southern Africa. This line drawing, by Lance Penny, is a reconstruction of the town centre, with the commoners living at the bottom of the hill, royalty on the high terraces, and the king on top.

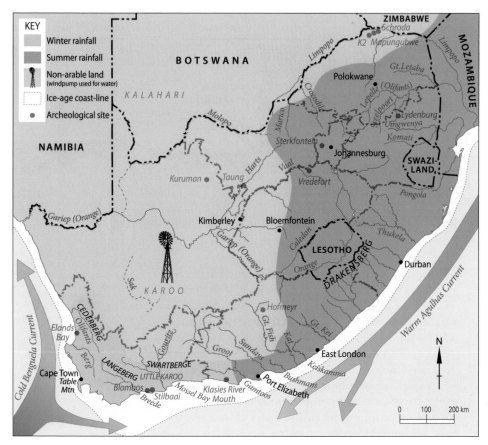

KEY
- Winter rainfall
- Summer rainfall
- Non-arable land (windpump used for water)
- Ice-age coast-line
- Archeological site

Water in South African history. Summer rain; winter rain; almost no rain: these have been the realities of life for people living in South Africa for thousands of years. Rivers have played a major role. And the coastline has shrunk as the ice locked up in the polar caps 20 000 years ago melted and the level of the sea rose 120 metres.

Africa, also bringing with them grain and cattle, and a knowledge of iron working and pottery making. They eventually settled on the well-watered coastal belt of what is today KwaZulu-Natal and the Eastern Cape. They were followed 200 to 300 years later by further newcomers, who settled on the high ground in the centre and north of the country and who spoke the ancestral Sotho-Tswana languages.

Quite how far south the Nguni speakers had moved by the 11th or 12th centuries is not yet certain, but by the 16th century they were established at the Kei River and may well already have been living along the Gamtoos River, just west of present-day Port Elizabeth, where the summer rainfall region ends. There is some information available about the nature of the interaction between the San and these immigrants from the north, whose farming skills enabled settlement and thus a more complex level of social organisation than was possible for hunter–gatherers. San artefacts and paintings would suggest that at the time the San occupied most of the land. And whilst they were displaced from much of it, there is plenty of evidence to suggest that there was also a great deal of close interaction. Genetic analysis shows the incorporation of Khoe ancestry into several of the south-east Bantu populations c.1 500–1 000 years ago. The three different clicks in isiXhosa were clearly acquired from close contact with the San over a long period of time. Marked San features, such as high cheekbones, are also clearly visible in many isiXhosa speakers, including, most famously, Nelson Mandela.

First invented in the United States in the middle of the 19th century, these metal windpumps were introduced into South Africa during the time of the mineral discoveries and spread throughout the drier parts of the country (marked in yellow on the map opposite) as an integral part of the country's industrial revolution.

5

EUROPE RETURNS TO SUB-SAHARAN AFRICA: 1488–1806

More than 50000 years were to pass before human beings, who had first walked out of Africa to inhabit the rest of the world, came back to the southern tip of Africa, where long-established hunters and gatherers (San) as well as pastoral people with cattle and sheep (Khoe) were living. Desire for gold and spices were two of the major factors that drove the bold seafarers of the Mediterranean to venture far from home during the 15th century. After rounding the Cape, the Portuguese established themselves in India and south-east Asia at the beginning of the 16th century, but in southern Africa it was not for another century and a half that a European maritime power would decide to establish a permanent presence. In 1652 Jan van Riebeeck was sent by the Dutch to set up a refreshment station halfway on the arduous sea journey to the East Indies. And so began the long, turbulent process of colonisation …

A painting from the journals of the Dutch soldier, explorer and artist Robert Gordon, who travelled widely through South Africa. He was stationed at the Cape, where he commanded the Dutch garrison for 15 years until the first British occupation in 1795.

A Portuguese sailing ship of the 15th century. The initial voyages from Europe were taken by Portugal and Spain (although the Italian, Christopher Columbus played a hugely significant role). In one memorable decade, starting in 1488, the Portuguese rounded the Cape at the southern tip of Africa, the Spanish reached America, and the Pope brokered a treaty between the two maritime powers that divided 'the world of new discoveries' either side of a vertical line drawn through the middle of the Atlantic. Unbeknown to anybody at the time, a significant portion of South America jutted east into the Atlantic across the Pope's line, which meant, in due course, that Portugal, rather than Spain, acquired the sanction to colonise Brazil, in addition to Africa and lands further to the east.

ONE SUMMER'S DAY IN 1488, A GROUP OF KHOE, grazing their cattle by the sea near today's Mossel Bay, saw something most unusual. A huge object moved through the waves. Men, pale-skinned and speaking a strange language, landed to collect water. The local people threw stones at these strange men, who in turn shot one of the Khoe with a crossbow before sailing away. Further up the coast, Bartholomew Dias would plant a cross near the Bushman's River mouth before his mutinous crew forced him to turn around and sail for home – but he had paved the way. Nine years later another ship arrived. The meeting was more friendly. Water and meat were provided and the captain joined the dancing before continuing his voyage. Vasco da Gama was thus the first man to reach India by sailing round the notoriously treacherous Cape of Storms, as Dias had named it. It was also, however, called the Cape of Good Hope, as it opened the sea route from Europe to the East. In his classic study on the causes of the wealth of nations, Adam Smith sees this voyage as one of the two most significant voyages in history, the other being Columbus's successful crossing from Europe to North America in 1492.

At first, the Portuguese were determined to find a sea route to the source of the gold that was coming across the Sahara from West Africa on camels driven by Muslim traders. It took them two generations to establish the sea route down the west coast of Africa and during this time their goals changed. On the islands of Madeira and São Tomé they discovered that they could grow sugar and, on the mainland, that they could capture or buy slaves to work in their sugar plantations. Then spices beckoned. If they could sail around Africa, across to India and then down to the clove islands of south Asia, they could control the lucrative trade which at that time involved a hazardous overland route to Venice.

For those living on the southern coast of Africa, the next visitors were more troublesome. In 1510 a ship with the Portuguese viceroy of India on board sailed into Table Bay. His men behaved provocatively and the Khoe drove them back to their boat, killing 65, including the viceroy. Subsequently, many of the passing ships gave the Cape of Storms a wide berth. By the turn of the 17th century, Holland had muscled in on the spice trade and had gained sufficient naval dominance in the Indian Ocean to establish the East India Trading Company (known as the Vereenigde

Vasco da Gama, Portuguese mariner, who in 1497 captained the first ship to sail from Europe to India.

Dutch sailing ships of the 17th century.

Sir John Barrow's frontispiece of a slave being flogged at the Cape was torn from many of the extant copies of his account of travels into the interior of South Africa (1801–1804).

Oost-Indische Compagnie, or VOC). To ensure a regular supply of vegetables, meat and water to ships making the long voyage around the Cape, the VOC sent a party of men and women to occupy the Cape Peninsula and to build a fort, today known as The Castle in Cape Town.

> [We] observed that on the ascent of Table Mountain the pasture was everywhere crowded with cattle and sheep like grass on the fields, which the said captains [of the Saldaniers, a Khoe people] gave us to understand was theirs, and that they intended to bring their houses close by and reside here … the Saldaniers … lay in thousands about Salt River with their cattle in countless numbers, having indeed grazed 2 000 sheep and cattle within half a cannon-shot of our fort.
>
> *Jan van Riebeeck, commander of the first party to land at the Cape, soon after his arrival in 1652*

The fort was built, at first, of mud, but neither the Khoe nor the San had the military power to drive the Europeans away. They were defeated by a combination of disease and guns. In 1687 a fever epidemic took a great toll. Outbreaks of smallpox were yet more devastating, first in 1713 and again in 1755. The Khoe showed considerable resistance, culminating in a major battle in 1739 some 100 miles north of Cape Town

where the Dutch farmers ('Trekboers') had claimed farm land. By this stage the Khoesan – the Khoe had seemingly fused with the San in this part of South Africa – caused nearly 50 farms to be abandoned and made off with nearly 3 000 sheep and 700 cattle as they sought to push the invaders south of the Berg River. Subsequently, a commando attacked a Khoesan stronghold in the mountains, but retreated under a hail of arrows. Further north, along the boundary between winter- and summer-rainfall regions, where both domestic and wild animals could survive the dry seasons, the land was strongly contested for 100 years by Trekboers, Khoe pastoralists and San hunters.

Gradually arrivals from Europe moved deeper into southern Africa. In 1786 Graaff-Reinet was established 600 km from Cape Town to support military forces fighting on two fronts. Neither the San (to the north) nor the Xhosa (to the east) accepted the European assumption that the land was theirs for the taking. Conflict with the San became acute. Between 1785 and 1795, for example, 2 504 San were killed and 669 captured in raiding parties. One particularly haunting aspect of this systematic extermination of the San

In the 19th century in England, it was fashionable to decorate a book on its fore-edge (the front side of the text-block situated between the covers and opposite the spine). Shown here is a fore-edge painting of Table Bay which appears on a book published in 1815.

The abundant wildlife reported all over southern Africa by early European travellers was decimated – and in many places rapidly exterminated – in the decades after the arrival of guns from Europe. This painting from Robert Gordon's journal depicts a hippo hunt.

by European invaders was that they were in a sense destroying their own ancestry.

Natural population growth in the new settlement was augmented by two streams of immigrants: slaves from other parts of Africa (especially Madagascar) and south-east Asia; and refugees from Europe, including nearly 300 French Huguenots, most of them arriving in 1688. Although they lost their language, many of the refugees acquired land in Franschhoek and elsewhere, and, with their wine-growing skills, laid the basis of one of the Cape's first export industries. The history of the slaves is very different. Although the Khoe did barter animals, which the VOC needed to replenish passing ships, neither they nor the San were prepared to work in significant numbers for the new arrivals. Thus the Dutch turned, just as the English were doing in the sugar plantations of Barbados, to the slave trade the Portuguese had pioneered soon after they first ventured down the west coast of Africa. A ship, on its way to Brazil from Angola, was captured in 1658, and thus the first 75 slaves landed in Cape Town.

Over the next 150 years, 65 000 slaves were brought to the Cape. In the end, two-thirds of them came from Madagascar, but many originated in Angola, Mozambique and in the Indonesian islands of Java (then Batavia) and elsewhere. Many were Muslim. By 1700 there were more slaves than colonists. Robert Shell writes that the Cape had become '[a] slave society … in which all institutions – the labour market, the economy, the legal system, the family and the church – are permeated by slavery. The master–slave model served as the model for all other relationships'.

What do we know about life at this time north and east of the Cape? Occasional survivors from shipwrecks in the 16th and 17th centuries wrote about well-ordered communities on the eastern seaboard of the country. In the 18th century scientists from Europe became fascinated by the country. In 1705 Peter Kolb, trained in mathematics and medicine, came from Germany to the Cape. He stayed for eight years and was the first to publish a comprehensive list of the country's fauna – mammals, birds, fish, snakes and insects. He did not, it seems, move far beyond Cape Town. Two Swedish naturalists, Carl Peter Thunberg and Anders Sparrman were the first in a long line of distinguished scientists who were to travel widely in South Africa during the 18th and 19th centuries and who, along with Kolb, would lay the foundations of a strong scientific tradition that has made major contributions to knowledge in many fields, ranging from astronomy, botany and cartography, through geology and palaeontology, to zoology. At the same time, a colourful French ornithologist, François Le Vaillant, set off on a journey

Trade at the foot of Table Mountain, c.1710. Tools and trinkets from Europe were exchanged for the meat and ivory of Africa.

A painting by François Le Vaillant, French adventurer, artist and ornithologist, of his camp on the Great Fish River, c.1785.

Georg Schmidt.

Johannes van der Kemp.

that he vividly recorded both in words and paintings. Conscious of the sense of social injustice that was soon to fuel the French Revolution, he grew close to the Khoe servants with whom he travelled and enjoyed meeting parties of Khoe and Xhosa along the way. He christened a beautiful Khoe girl he met on the banks of the Great Fish River Nerine, after an indigenous flower, and named a particularly bright and rare bird the Narina Trogon in her honour. He was scathing about the predatory behaviour of the Dutch settlers with regard to the indigenous people.

But perhaps the most remarkable of the scientists to visit during this period was the botanist William Burchell, who spent nearly four years travelling through the country before returning to England with over 63 000 objects 'in every branch of natural history', including meticulously collected botanical specimens, animal skins, birds and several hundred drawings. Later Charles Darwin himself visited the Cape near the end of his voyage on the *Beagle*.

Contrasting with the behaviour of the European colonists described by Le Vaillant, a German named George Schmidt landed at the Cape in 1737. Schmidt was a Moravian missionary and established himself on the banks of the Riviersonderend ('River without end') 150 km east of Cape Town, where he preached to the Khoe and taught people to read. After seven years he was driven out of the country by the combined hostility of the local farmers and the Dutch Reformed predikante (ministers) in Cape Town. However, 50 years later, new

Moravian missionaries arrived, found one of Schmidt's converts still alive and re-established the mission. They renamed it Genadendal ('Vale of Mercy') and it came to play a key role in both missionary work and the broader education of South Africa. It was there, in 1799, that Johannes van der Kemp of the London Missionary Society came to prepare for his journey to meet King Ngqika and to work amongst the Xhosa and, later, the Khoe. Genadendal also provided an inspiration for others, including Robert Moffat (who established the

Genadendal Mission was founded in 1738 on the banks of the Riviersonderend, 150 km east of Cape Town.

General J W Janssens, the Dutch governor of the Cape in the period between the first and second British occupations, travelled to the eastern part of the country. In 1803, on the west bank of the Kat River, he met King Ngqika of the Xhosa.

influential mission at Kuruman, where the first school north of the Orange River was built in 1829) and John Ross (who arrived with a printing press in his luggage and stayed for some days – taking careful notes – on his way to the eastern Cape, where he and John Bennie were to found Lovedale in 1824). Many of the missionaries were remarkable human beings whose work, over the next century, was to have a major impact on the lives of local people.

Meanwhile, the turmoil in Europe set in train by the

Cape Town's Strand and Burg streets in the 18th century, during the period of rule by the Dutch East India Company (voc), shown in a watercolour by Samuel Davis.

French Revolution of 1789 became visible in the Cape, whence the British, disturbed by France's expansion in Europe – which included an attack on Holland – sent a fleet south in 1795 to take over from the Dutch garrison in Cape Town. The British occupation of the Cape lasted for eight years, until they relinquished control to the Dutch (Batavian Republic) in 1803. But, with renewed concern about French intentions under Napoleon, the British re-occupied the Cape in 1806. With this, the rising imperial power took a firm grip on the colony it was to rule for the next century.

6

AMBIGUOUS EMPIRE: 1806–1879

The second British occupation of the Cape, beginning in 1806, marked a turning point in South Africa's history and in its relationship with the wider world. In the previous century and a half of occupation by the Dutch, hardly any roads had been built, but within their first 30 years, the British, with the help of their troops, had built roads across the Cape Peninsula as well as an all-important pass across the ring of mountains which separated it from the rest of the country. At the same time, powerful British forces were sent to the eastern frontier where conflict over land threatened to destabilise an uneasy peace. A reluctant imperialist? Hardly. During the course of the 19th century Great Britain was drawn inexorably into the swirling processes of conflict and cooperation that characterised South Africa. The two generations before the discovery of diamonds, which opened a new chapter in the country's history, were to prove crucial in shaping the South Africa that was to emerge as the continent's leading industrial power in the 20th century.

In a visit to South Africa in the middle of the 19th century, Thomas Baines travelled widely and painted many vivid scenes, including several battles. Here we see the 74th Highlanders storming Wolf Ridge in the Amatole Mountains, where King Sandile was marshalling his forces in the war of 1850–1853.

THE EARLY YEARS OF BRITISH RULE WERE DRAMATIC. British soldiers, in moves reminiscent of the Highland Clearances in Scotland (where English troops had forcefully moved people off the land to create space for commercial sheep farming), were sent to the eastern Cape to push the Xhosa off all land west of the Great Fish River. This was led, ironically, by a Scot – Colonel John Graham – using what the British governor, Sir John Cradock, called 'a proper degree of terror'. The onslaught of 1812 was followed by a crucial battle in Grahamstown in 1819, when the Xhosa, led by Makanda, very nearly defeated the British. However, their attack was repulsed and they were pushed still further east. The following year the British government brought in 4 000 people from England and settled them on the land from which the Xhosa had been evicted.

The Xhosa, devastated by their loss of land and cattle, took 15 years to gather sufficient forces to sweep

Xhosa warriors (below right).

Prince Maqoma (below) was the most skilful of the Xhosa military leaders during the hundred years' war of dispossession on the eastern frontier. His guerrilla campaign in the thick forests of the Waterkloof near the Kat River tied down the British forces for months during the bitter war of 1850–1853.

across the frontier in retaliation. Again they were defeated by superior arms, but they continued to resist strongly and, led by Prince Maqoma, to wage guerrilla war against British forces. In one last desperate sacrificial move to stop the white juggernaut, many clans – urged by a young female soothsayer, Nonqawuse – killed their cattle and decided not to plant crops in order to appease the ancestors. To no avail. By late summer of 1857 starvation stalked the land. But the Xhosa, unlike the Irish in the great famine a few years earlier, could not emigrate. The only solution lay in finding jobs, if they could, on the farms that the invaders were staking out in the south. During this process some 300 farms were set aside for white occupation between the Great Fish and the Keiskamma Rivers and over 2000 German settlers – originally recruited to fight for Britain in the Crimean War, a conflict which ended before they could be deployed – were brought in by the British governor.

King Shaka, north of the Thukela River in Zululand, built an army – trained with extraordinary discipline and using new methods of fighting with short-handled spears – that swept all before it.

The interior of the country was the scene of turbulence and conflict throughout the 19th century as people fought for land, and accordingly advanced or retreated. This huge movement of the various populations was known as the Difaqane ('the Scattering'). In part of what is today KwaZulu-Natal, the powerful Zulu king Shaka was establishing a military kingdom. Many people, including refugees or 'mfengu', fled to the eastern Cape. The Ndebele, led by Mzilikazi, established themselves aggressively on the Highveld, between the Vaal and Limpopo rivers. More pressure was added by

This painting by Thomas Baines shows one of the many battles between Zulu and European invaders – both Dutch and British – during the 19th century. Here, at Blaaukrantz in 1838, Zulu impis attacked Voortrekker wagons near what later became Weenen or 'Place of Weeping'.

King Cetshwayo inherited Shaka's army and was able to inflict a bruising defeat on the British at Isandlwana in 1879. But, in the end, the gun was mightier than the spear – and the Zulu were defeated.

the arrival of Dutch-speaking Voortrekkers ('Pioneers') who had decided to leave the Cape Colony in angry defiance of the British. They bitterly resented not only Ordinance 50 of 1828, which sought to protect the rights of the Khoe, but also the British governor's pro-English language policy. The abolition of slavery finally convinced them that they had to establish their independence elsewhere.

Their slow progress north – known as the Great Trek – brought them into the territory of the Ndebele. Attack and counterattack followed until the Ndebele moved north to carve out an enclave in part of what is now Zimbabwe. Another party of Voortrekkers had penetrated into Zulu-dominated territory, provoking a fierce and prolonged clash. But the guns of industrial

Europe defeated the spears and courage of the Zulu impis at a major battle on the Ncome River (subsequently known in colonial history as Blood River). The British then moved in and annexed Natal in 1843. Within a decade some 5 000 immigrants had arrived from Europe and settled in the new colony.

A generation later Zulu opposition to European invasion was dramatically demonstrated at the Battle of Isandlwana in January 1879, when, after concealing themselves brilliantly, Zulu King Cetshwayo's army of 20 000 men routed the British. But the victory was short-lived and by July of that year the Zulu Kingdom had been destroyed.

Meanwhile in the high interior the Sotho, under their remarkable king, Moshoeshoe, took refuge in the Maluti Mountains, near present-day Lesotho, using the western escarpment of the Drakensberg as a

King Moshoeshoe mustered an army of 10 000 mounted men equipped with firearms to defeat Boer invaders at Thaba Bosiu in 1858. Ten years later, after appeals by Moshoeshoe for protection, the British governor of the Cape annexed Lesotho as an independent colony.

At the Battle of Isandlwana the Zulu army's mastery of the terrain enabled them to attack the British troops and take them by surprise.

Robert Moffat preaching to the Coranna chief Mosheu and his people about 200 km from Kuruman, c.1834.

Piet Retief, a farmer from the eastern Cape, was one of the leaders of the Great Trek. He was killed at a meeting – which he thought was for purposes of negotiation – with King Dingane of the Zulu.

fortress. In 1858, 10 000 armed Sotho horsemen drove off invading Boer commandos, but seven years later Moshoeshoe, now an old man, was defeated. He was, however, able to negotiate with the British for protection for some land, which now makes up Lesotho. In the process, much of the most fertile land west of the Caledon River was lost to the invading Dutch farmers. These Voortrekkers, led by Hendrik Potgieter and others, were staking out land for themselves across the Orange and the Vaal rivers. They set up independent republics that were recognised by the British government in the 1850s. The Orange Free State, with its capital in Bloemfontein, maintained its sovereignty for half a century, whilst the Zuid-Afrikaansche Republiek (or ZAR, later known as the Transvaal) had a more chequered career. Annexed as a British colony in 1877, it initiated an armed rebellion which culminated in the defeat of imperial forces on Majuba Mountain in 1881.

North-east of these events, the Pedi, in a fertile crescent between two rivers, the Steelpoort and the Olifants, were gradually dispossessed of their land by a combination of Boer and British power (aided by Swazi reinforcements). 'My object,' noted Sir Garnet Wolseley in 1879, in words strikingly similar to those used two generations earlier by Sir John Cradock in the eastern Cape, 'is to strike terror into the hearts of the surrounding tribes by the utter destruction of Sikukuni [King Sekhukhune], root and branch …'

For the Bantu-speaking peoples, these were times of bitter defeat. Desperately defending their land, Xhosa, Sotho, Zulu, Ndebele, Pedi, Venda and others were to be overwhelmed by the combination of British Redcoats and Boer commandos. Yet, paradoxically, there were also the fragile beginnings of a process that would transform the conquered societies and lay the foundations of eventual liberation to democracy – that is, through education.

The role of missionaries in South African history has been ambiguous, but their contribution to schooling has been immense. The first missionary to live amongst the Xhosa, Joseph Williams, settled to preach on the banks of the Kat River with his wife and baby son in 1816 and made a lasting impression not least on one man, Ntsikana, who wrote a great hymn that is sung to this day, and who came to symbolise the acceptance of modernity by Africans, through Christianity.

Sir Garnet Wolseley.

King Sekhukhune of the Pedi.

Ferry on the Berg River, by William Burchell. Before bridges, most of which were built in the 20th century, crossing the many rivers of South Africa was a time-consuming and hazardous process.

Subsequently the Xhosa language was written down and printed by Scots missionaries in the Tyhume Valley. Their most famous school, at Lovedale, was founded in 1841, and for the next century provided rigorous education for both black and white pupils. From Adams College near Durban to Zonnebloem in Cape Town, the mission schools – until they were all destroyed or crippled by apartheid's policy of Bantu Education in the 1950s – educated generations of the new African leadership, such as Thabo Mbeki and Chris Hani, as well as a host of remarkable women, including Ellen Kuzwayo.

Despite population migration and sporadic warfare across the country, and despite the fact that transport remained rudimentary, with ox wagons creaking slowly to and from the interior on bad roads, South Africa's economy began to expand. Much production was provided by subsistence farming, although wine had long been established as an export from the western Cape, whilst wheat and vegetables were also grown commercially. One of the first acts of the imperial government in 1813 was to limit farm size and to charge a 'quitrent' to encourage productive farming. The crop that was to propel South African agriculture into the global economy was wool. From the 1820s the number of Spanish merino sheep, imported from Australia, expanded rapidly. In Natal sugar plantations flourished: this was largely due to the twin help of a protective imperial-preference tariff and the arrival, in

The Girls' School at Lovedale in 1890. From the time it began in 1841, with 11 black and 9 white pupils, education at Lovedale was non-racial for a century. Many distinguished South Africans, both men and women, were educated there. The building shown in this photograph is today a ruin.

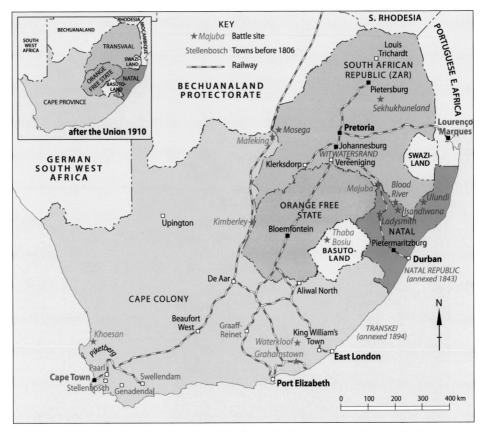

KEY

★ *Majuba* Battle site

Stellenbosch Towns before 1806

▬▬▬ Railway

South Africa in the 19th century. After the British took control of the Cape in 1806, the map of South Africa began to change dramatically. New towns were established along the coast and then inland, first by the Voortrekkers and then by those in search of minerals. In the 30 years after the discovery of diamonds in 1867, some 4 000 miles of railway line were laid in a country where previously ox wagons and horses had been the only forms of transport.

1860, of Indian indentured labourers, some 150000 of whom would be brought to the country over the next 50 years. Many Indian merchant families also came to South Africa during this period and were to add greatly to the rich diversity of the country.

The centre of gravity within the government began to shift. From rule largely by officials responsible to London, authority in the Cape moved after 1853 to a parliament elected on a franchise open to any adult male inhabitant above a certain property or income threshold. Non-racial in theory, practice meant that whites never constituted less than 85% of the electorate and produced 100% of the MPs. Nevertheless, a block of no more than 15% of votes could not be completely ignored in the public discourse. In Natal whites had, in practice, 100% of the franchise. And in the two Voortrekker republics the founders had always been explicit in their rejection of any equality between black and white.

7

BLACK, WHITE & GOLD – INDUSTRIAL REVOLUTION: 1867–1947

The discovery of diamonds 1 000 km north of Cape Town in 1867 and then of gold nearby 19 years later generated a fever of excitement as people rushed in from around the world – and from all over southern Africa – to seek their fortunes. Investment poured in and the industrial revolution which was to transform the country was soon well under way. A century before the spectacular economic growth of a number of Asian countries, South Africa was to become one of the first of the so-called Newly Industrialising Countries, famous for its rapid economic growth from a standing start. By 1899 nearly 4 000 miles of railway line had been laid, ensuring cheap and rapid transport from the harbour cities, where the shipping lines ended, to the mining towns that had sprung up virtually overnight. Johannesburg was a city in a hurry: within ten years of its founding it was larger than Cape Town, which was then 250 years old.

Song of the Pick, by Gerard Sekoto (1919–1993), was painted in 1946–7.

Cecil Rhodes, who died at the age of 49, packed several lifetimes of work into the 30 years he spent in South Africa. He made a fortune out of diamonds and gold; helped to establish the migrant labour system; became prime minister of the Cape; and drove north the railway through Bechuanaland (Botswana) – avoiding Kruger's Transvaal – to open up the two countries that were to bear his name for much of the 20th century.

Alfred Milner.

DIAMONDS IN KIMBERLEY PAVED THE WAY, BUT IT was to be gold-mining – pioneered by the young Cecil Rhodes, who had come from England to seek his fortune and had accumulated the necessary capital from diamond profits – that was to be the real engine of the new economy. Here, wrote the South African historian Cornelis de Kiewiet in a much quoted passage,

was an industry which feared neither locusts nor cattle diseases, neither drought nor summer floods. Its product always commanded a ready sale in the financial centres of the world … Gold, in consequence, did many things for South Africa. It stabilized revenues and preserved national income from violent fluctuations. It gave firmness to foreign trade because it was by far the principal article of export … Like a great flywheel the mining industry gave stability to a country that otherwise would have been singularly sensitive to movements in world economy. Farming, so sensitive to world conditions without, and to drought and pestilence within, found comfort and strength in the lee of the Witwatersrand.

Agriculture did indeed blossom. New markets in the middle of the country, combined with railways, transformed the farming sector. With the help of subsidies generated by the mines and favourable protection from the state, South Africa was to become one of the few countries in the world which regularly exported food, and this despite its poor and erratic rainfall. After diamonds and gold came coal, iron ore, copper: South Africa was to prove extraordinarily rich in minerals.

Immigrants poured in from all sides. One particularly important group, pushed out by the political upheavals of central Europe, where pogroms had been unleashed by the assassination of the Russian tsar, Nicholas II, in 1881, and pulled by the new wealth of southern Africa, were Jews. Many came from Lithuania. Before that time there had been fewer than 500 Jews in South Africa, but by 1910 40000 had migrated to South Africa. Over the course of the next three generations, they were to play a role, out of all proportion to their numbers, in commerce, art, politics and law.

The forging of the new industrial state did not happen without bitter conflict. In 1899 Great Britain provoked the ZAR, led by Paul Kruger and supported by the Orange Free State, into war. The fundamental reason was British desire to control the goldfields and a long-felt urge to bring the independent-minded Boers under their authority. This proved to be difficult. Although the British entered the two capitals of Pretoria and Bloemfontein within seven months, they found that the war was by no means over. Harried on all sides by accurate guerrilla marksmen on swift horses, the British resorted to war against civilians. Crops and homesteads were burnt throughout the countryside whilst women and children were rounded up into concentration camps. Nearly 28000 Boers – 80% of them children and, of the adults, two-thirds women – perished in the camps. In addition, of the

As a boy, Paul Kruger travelled with the Voortrekker wagons as they moved deeper into Africa. As president of the ZAR (subsequently the Transvaal) he was to become the most formidable of the Boer leaders in the struggle against British imperialism. He left the ZAR just before the British occupation of Pretoria to seek help abroad and died in Switzerland in 1904.

John Tengo Jabavu and his son Professor D D T Jabavu each played prominent roles in the public life of South Africa over a period that spanned 60 turbulent years, from the founding of the isiXhosa newspaper *Imvo Zabantsundu* (by John Tengo) in 1884 to the leadership of the All Africa Convention (by Prof. D D T), which fought against the 1936 legislation removing Africans in the Cape from the common voters' roll.

115 000 black South Africans interned in camps, 20 000 died. Although the final peace treaty gave the former republics the whites-only franchise they wanted, the net result of the war was to generate a passionate anti-British, Afrikaner nationalism which grew steadily in strength until, in 1948, it came to power under the banner of apartheid.

After the war the British high commissioner, Lord Milner, appointed a commission to look into the future of Africans in South Africa. This body, composed entirely of whites – most of them English-speaking – and chaired by Sir Godfrey Lagden, wrote a report which was to serve as a blueprint for South African policy-making over the next 80 years. At its heart was the principle of territorial segregation based on race, with whites owning the lion's share of the land.

But the story was not simply in black and white. For as the mines moved into full post-war production, the shortage of unskilled labour was so acute (black wages had been lowered during the war) that the mining industry, in collaboration with the British government, organised widespread recruiting in China. As a result, some 64 000 young Chinese workers were brought in to work on the gold mines on three-year contracts. Due to vociferous opposition in Britain, these contracts were not renewed, as originally planned, and by 1910 all Chinese mineworkers had been sent home. There was also, during this period, a significant presence of Chinese merchants, some of whom became active in protesting against discriminatory legislation.

In 1910, soon after the Lagden Commission issued its influential report, the former colonies and republics came together as the Union of South Africa – a compromise agreement, essentially, to unite the white populace. They took little heed of strong opposition – from African and coloured leaders (including John Tengo Jabavu and Dr Abdurahman) and supported by two former prime ministers of the Cape (Sir Gordon Sprigg and W P Schreiner) – to the introduction of new (and entrenchment of old) colour bars in the constitution of the country. The Union was soon tested by the outbreak of the First World War in 1914, when Boer veterans rose in short-lived rebellion against two of their former generals, Louis Botha and Jan Smuts, who had led South Africa into the War alongside Great Britain. There followed four painful years, during which over 7000 South Africans, both white and black, lost their lives.

A sharp fall in the price of gold in 1922 led to an armed rebellion by white miners supported by the recently founded South African Communist Party (SACP). They were incensed at management's attempt to cut costs by breaching the colour bar and replacing them with black workers at lower wages. Although the Rand Rebellion was rapidly put down by armed troops, the white miners won the war and the colour bar was effectively entrenched within the industry for the next half-century. The rise in the price of gold, following Roosevelt's devaluation of the dollar in 1933, and the subsequent expansion both of mining and of

Dr Abdullah Abdurahman, medical doctor and political thinker.

Louis Botha, Boer general and first prime minister of the Union of South Africa from 1910 to 1919.

'n Boer maak 'n plan ('A Boer makes a plan'). Crossing a river, 1926.

secondary industry, enabled South Africa to weather the worst of the Great Depression.

This process of industrialisation was accompanied by urbanisation, as people were drawn to the towns by new jobs and pushed out of the rural areas by drought, population growth and agricultural mechanisation. For blacks this painful process was exacerbated by the loss of much of their land through conquest: a loss entrenched by the Land Act of 1913, which prohibited them from owning land in most of the country and which established reserves – areas not yet colonised by white farmers – for black occupation. These reserves were to become the 'Homelands' or Bantustans (later the 'Black States') of apartheid South Africa.

By 1904, nearly a quarter of the total population – only 10% of blacks but more than half the whites – was already living in urban areas. By 1936 the proportion had risen to nearly a third (31%), and by 1960 to nearly a half (47%). After the First World War, gross national product (GDP) rose by an average of 5% per annum for 30 years – enough to ensure a steady growth in average per capita real income despite increasing population. In economic terms South Africa's industrial revolution, culminating in the manufacturing expansion triggered by the Second World War, looked like a success. But only at first glance.

For underneath the gleaming railway tracks and rising skyscrapers of a modern industrial economy

A 'poor-white' family in 1926. Poverty endured by whites pushed off the land by a variety of forces and ill-equipped to compete for jobs in the new urban environment became a major political issue in the decades after the South African War.

Handlashing into a truck deep down a gold mine.

were three or four fundamental weaknesses which lay like seismic faults waiting to erupt. The men who gained control of the diamond diggings in Kimberley after 1867 were determined to prevent their employees from trading any diamonds found. To this end they introduced strip-searching. In 1884 the white miners went on strike and marched in protest. Six men were shot dead by police – but miners were never strip-searched again. Black miners, however, were powerless to prevent being compulsorily housed in closed, single-sex compounds on the mine which they could only leave at the end of their contract after having been strip-searched.

UNDERGROUND WORK

South Africans are good at underground work – not only of the political kind.

- Mine shafts have been drilled down to levels of more than 3 km below the surface of the earth and hundreds of kilometres of tunnels have been dug in pursuit of gold since 1886.
- An excavator shield, designed by James Henry Greathead, a young engineer from the eastern Cape, enabled London to dig the world's first underground railway system at the end of the 19th century. The same technology was subsequently used in Paris, New York and Moscow.

- The Great Escape, in which hundreds of prisoners of war in the Nazi Stalag Luft III camp near Zagan in Poland dug three tunnels, thus enabling 76 airmen to escape in 1944, was conceived and led by a young South African-born RAF pilot, Roger Bushell, who was himself the son of the manager of one of the gold mines on the Rand, east of Johannesburg.

From the time of the mineral discoveries until the abolition of passes in 1986, few cash-earning jobs were open to African women apart from domestic service. Whether on the commercial farms or in the growing cities (when they were allowed to be there), African women worked largely as cleaners, cooks and childminders (or 'nannies') for white families.

Again, when gold was discovered and 50 000 miners were needed quickly, the new magnates took from Kimberley not only their profits to finance the new mines, but also the labour model which had served them so well. Compounds were built to accommodate black workers, who were then recruited from far afield. Between 1896 and 1946 the number of black miners rose from 54 000 to 305 000. No less than 60% of the miners in 1896 came from Mozambique, whilst by 1946 the main areas supplying labour were Mozambique (32%), the eastern Cape (28%), Lesotho (13%) and Malawi (11%). Thus was the migrant labour system, drawing mineworkers on a temporary basis not only from the rural areas of the country, but also from far beyond its political boundaries, embedded in the heart of South Africa's industrial revolution.

Closely related to labour was land policy. Legislation in 1913 decreed that no land owned by whites could be bought by blacks; black ownership of land was

Colleagues in war and peace, Jan Smuts succeeded Louis Botha as prime minister of South Africa. He served twice, in 1919–1924 and 1939–1948, and was also in the British War Cabinet in both World Wars. A man of many parts, Smuts was a philosopher as well as an environmentalist ahead of his time.

largely communal, confined to those areas which had not yet been turned into white-owned commercial farms. Eventually, these 'native reserves' constituted no more than 13.7% of the area of South Africa; they were too overpopulated for agricultural purposes and effectively served as labour reserves for mining and other sectors of the growing economy.

The third prong of these policies was manifest, as noted above, in regulations to protect white workers from being undercut in the workplace either by better skills or lower wages – or both. In 1911, for example, the Mines and Works Act made it illegal for black miners to hold blasting certificates, thus ensuring that black miners, no matter how skilled, were unable to rise up the job hierarchy. This policy was reinforced and extended during the 1920s and 1930s by the so-called 'Civilised Labour' policy, which ensured that white workers were employed ahead of black workers in the railways, the civil service and the iron and steel industry.

THE WORLD'S JEWELLERY BOX

For over 100 years – until it was overtaken by China in 2007 – South Africa was the leading gold producer in the world. It remains the number one producer of aluminosilicates, ferrochromium, the platinum group of minerals, vanadium and vermiculite – and has the world's largest reserve base of chrome ore. It is the world's second biggest producer not only of gold, but also of manganese ore and titanium minerals. It remains amongst the world's top ten in the production of a host of other minerals, including antimony, coal, diamonds, ferromanganese, ferrosilicon, fluorspar, iron ore, nickel, phosphate rock and silicon metal.

Sol Plaatje's book *Native Life in South Africa* (1916) provided vivid evidence of the harsh consequences for black South Africans of the introduction of the Land Act of 1913. Plaatje became the first general-secretary of the South African Native National Congress (SANNC), which would later become the ANC. His novel *Mhudi* (1930), originally written in 1919, is believed to be the first novel by a black South African.

As the economy expanded during the Second World War, more and more black workers were drawn into the manufacturing industry, where the colour bar, whilst not as rigid as in the mines, was very real. The net result was that most of the wealth, both in the form of assets and of income, generated by South Africa's industrial revolution over 80 years from the time of the first mineral discoveries, remained firmly in white hands. In the gold mines, from 1911 to 1946, the average earnings of all white miners employed was roughly 12 times the average earnings of all black miners.

Another seismic fault underlying South Africa's pattern of economic growth was its long-term environmental impact. Considerable concern was expressed from time to time about soil erosion, the Drought Investigation Committee of 1922 warning that erosion could lead to 'national suicide'. But there was almost

Olive Schreiner, novelist and political writer.

no consciousness about the pollution of water sources by the mining industry.

The outbreak of the Second World War bitterly divided the white community between those who chose neutrality and those who followed General Smuts into alliance with Britain. Black extra-parliamentary solidarity with the Atlantic Charter – in terms of which all peoples had a right to self-determination – resulted in many black South Africans joining the Allies. And although most black people were not allowed to bear arms, it is little known that more than 25% of the 5 500 South Africans killed during the War – in North Africa, Italy and elsewhere – were black.

Despite all the division during this period of industrialisation, a deeper sense of national solidarity was starting to crystallise as women and men drew on their roots to write novels, essays and poetry to express a new, consciously South African identity. Olive Schreiner's *The Story of an African Farm* (1883) came first, but her subsequent *Thoughts on South Africa* (1923), together with Sol Plaatje's *Native Life in South Africa* (1916) and poems such as Louis Leipoldt's *Oom Gert Vertel* (1911), along with SEK Mqhayi's *The Sinking of the Mendi* (1933), gave a foretaste of the extraordinary range of writing that was to emerge, in several languages, from South Africa during the 20th century.

8
APARTHEID: 1948-1986

The general election of 1948, which excluded as voters all South Africans of African or Indian origin, was won by the National Party (NP). It was supported primarily by white Afrikaans speakers, descendants of those defeated by the British in the bitter war of 1899–1902, and campaigned on a new concept of 'apartheid' or 'separateness'. For some, looking at the racism, segregation and control of black labour embedded in the South African political economy, apartheid was nothing new, simply a continuation – with one more turn of the capitalist screw, perhaps – of policies that had been relentlessly pursued by white colonists ever since they had landed on the shores of Table Bay three centuries previously. But for others the election results of 1948 were a disaster – a moment when white South Africa turned its back on the new world opening up after the Second World War to pursue instead a naked, legalised racism that drew its ideals from the Nazis. With hindsight it is possible to see that both views contained elements of truth.

Senior members of the National Party listen to speeches during the 50th anniversary celebrations of the Party at De Wildt, Transvaal (North-West Province), October 1964. Photograph by David Goldblatt.

SEGREGATION, OF COURSE, WAS NOT NEW. LORD Milner's Lagden Commission had spelt out the policy at the beginning of the century during the process of reconstruction after the South African War; and the Land Act of 1913 had laid the foundations on which apartheid's policy of 'separate development' was to be built. A colour bar enforced by law, by custom and by white trade-union pressure prevented black workers from occupying most skilled jobs apart from teaching, preaching and nursing. Most public facilities had always been segregated and social discrimination was rife. Marriage between black and white was prohibited. The hated pass laws, which controlled the movement of black South Africans by requiring all black men to carry documents authorising their movement from one place to another, went back in one form or another deep into the 19th century and had been made more

During the apartheid years the pass laws, which controlled the movement of black South Africans, became ever more stringent. By the early 1970s, more than 500 000 people were being arrested every year for being somewhere without the permission of the state.

rigorous soon after the mineral discoveries increased the demand for cheap labour.

Yet the election of 1948 presented white voters with a clear choice. Two reports published some months earlier proposed two very different policies for the future. The Fagan Commission appointed by the Smuts government, which had been in power throughout the Second World War, recognised the urbanisation of black South Africans that had taken place during this time and recommended the stabilisation of labour, which implied acceptance of the movement of black families from rural areas to live with their breadwinners. The Sauer Report, however, commissioned by the NP, which was led by Dr D F Malan, spelt out what apartheid would entail and proposed exactly the opposite. It went back to a policy formulated a generation previously by a local-government commission at the end of the First World War:

> The cities are the white man's creation and the black man may enter them so long as he ministers to the needs of the white man, but must depart therefrom when he ceases so to minister.

First of the prime ministers of the Union of South Africa who had not been a Boer general in the South African War, D F Malan was leader of a more exclusive Afrikaner nationalism which found expression in the policy of apartheid.

The apostles of apartheid, in effect, took the policy long pursued by the mining sector and applied it to the whole economy.

But the apartheid policy flew in the face of powerful socio-economic forces. For the country was industrialising at a rapid rate. Between 1904 and 1960 the

Accommodation in the all-male compounds of the mines and other sectors of South African industry improved over the years, but the old concrete bunks continued to be used in many places, as attested by this 1980 photograph.

proportion of total population living in towns rose from 23% to 47%; but, in racial terms, by 1960 over 80% of whites were urbanised, while only 32% of blacks were. This reflected previous anti-black urbanisation policies in the mines and elsewhere. It also meant that, by the time the apartheid government began to implement its policies, there were few white workers left in the rural areas to move to new jobs in the cities. The new labour would have to be black. The only way to resolve this contradiction was to enforce throughout the industrial economy the pattern of oscillating migration already established in the mining industry. This coercion was exerted through the pass laws which were steadily tightened and, in a bitterly resented move, extended to include African women.

The impact of the policy was devastating. Quite apart from turning the police into the enemy, the system of oscillating migration played havoc with family life as wives were separated from their husbands and fathers from their children. Moreover, it prevented women from moving to town and acquiring the skills needed to hold down urban jobs to supplement their meagre family incomes. And, over time, it reduced investment and production in the rural areas from which the migrants came. Thus, the pattern of industrialisation developed by the mining industry and extended by apartheid generated both wealth and poverty simultaneously. By the early 1970s it was estimated that one out of every two urban black workers was housed, as a migrant, in single-sex accommodation. In townships such as Langa in Cape Town, where the policy was rigorously applied, the ratio of men to women in 1974 was estimated to be eleven to one. Apartheid did more than divide black from white; it also divided the black man in half: labour unit in town, husband and father in the rural area.

Anti-black urbanisation was not the only distinguishing characteristic of apartheid. A second was the policy of what could be called 'ethnic cleansing'. Racist measures required that everybody be categorised into appropriate 'racial' groups. This led to the absurdities and indignities of the Population Registration Act, in terms of which thousands of people were reclassified each year according to rules that were without scientific or logical foundation. This process was directed primarily against black South Africans in rural areas and against those classified as 'Coloured' or 'Indian' in urban areas. Here and there a few whites were also moved to tidy things up for the apartheid planners. The individual consequences were often devastatingly cruel. The young schoolgirl Sandra Laing, for instance, born and brought up in a rural, white, Afrikaans-speaking family, was judged too dark to be white. She was removed from her school by her community and reclassified coloured. She left her family and later applied to be reclassified black so as to live in a community where she was accepted.

The most notorious of the urban removals were those of Sophiatown – home to many writers and musicians in Johannesburg – and of District Six, whence

A woman being man-handled by a policeman, almost certainly for not having her pass stamped with the necessary permission to be where she was.

Women's resistance to the pass laws throughout the 20th century was, if anything, even more determined than that of men. One of their leaders was Lilian Ngoyi.

60 000 people were bulldozed out of the heart of Cape Town. But there were many others who had to move. In the process, housing was often demolished, communities were broken up and people were forced to relocate miles away from where they worked. One of the main thrusts of this policy was to root out so-called 'black spots' in areas where black South Africans lived on land they had acquired, often through purchase before the Land Act of 1913 forbade such transactions. Others who had to move were people pushed off commercial farms by mechanisation and other pressures. Movement to town was forbidden and families were compelled to settle in the overcrowded Bantustans where there was no work. Described by a cabinet minister as 'surplus people', those forcibly resettled in this manner added up to more than 3 million people.

The third dimension of apartheid was perhaps the

Forced removals, which affected more than 3 million people, often damaged, if not destroyed, the asset base of people who did not have much to start with.

most radical. All South African governments subsequent to the Union in 1910 had pursued a policy of 'incorporation', whereby they attempted to bring the High Commission territories of Bechuanaland (Botswana), Basutoland (Lesotho) and Swaziland into the laager. But then, in 1958, one year after Kwame Nkrumah was elected president of an independent Ghana, Dr HF Verwoerd became prime minister. With African countries gaining independence one after the other, Britain found it expedient to advise South Africa that there was no chance of the three territories ever being handed over. Verwoerd tried one more time, before making a virtue of necessity by proclaiming that independence for African nations had been central to apartheid policy all along. South Africa supported the independence of Lesotho. Indeed, it would like to take the process further by giving independence to the Transkei and other parts of South Africa as well. Verwoerd persuaded the white electorate that a policy of dismembering the country into independent 'nations' would be a way of maintaining white control whilst providing space for the energies of African nationalism. Verwoerd well understood that, after a century supplying migrant labour to the mines of South Africa, Lesotho's internal capacity to generate wealth had effectively collapsed and the country's economic dependence on South Africa was so complete that it could never present a political threat. Moreover, the South African government could not be held responsible for pension payments, unemployment insurance or any public infrastructure that

Hendrik Verwoerd (at the microphone), chief architect of the policy of apartheid, was challenged on his home ground by the prime minister of Great Britain, Harold Macmillan, who addressed the South African parliament in February 1960 to warn of the 'wind of change' that was sweeping down Africa.

In a study of poverty in South Africa during the 1980s, it was found that rural households required two to three headloads of wood per week and that each headload, which averaged about 30 kg in weight, took anything from three to ten hours to collect.

people in the neighbouring state might need. From there it was but a short step to proclaiming independence for Transkei (1976), Bophuthatswana (1977), Venda (1979) and Ciskei (1981). Like characters from Alice's Wonderland, senior cabinet ministers of the apartheid government proclaimed solemnly in the 1980s that their goal was to ensure that there would be no black South Africans – as they would all become citizens of their own 'Homelands', or black national states.

But it was the fourth aspect of apartheid that was perhaps the most destructive. The Bantu Education Act of 1953 embodied a philosophy that specified that it would not educate black South Africans for positions in the economy beyond those they were expected to occupy. For Verwoerd, Minister of Native Affairs at the time, higher education for blacks, 'misled them by showing them the green pastures of European society in which they are not allowed to graze'. In practice this meant two things: first, that the great mission schools, which had been educating black South Africans for three or four generations, would either be closed or cease to function fully; and, second, that mathematics would no longer be taught as a core subject in black schools. Although the number of black children in school increased during the apartheid years, expenditure was kept to a fraction of that spent on white students and the quality of their education – not least the training of their teachers – lagged far behind. The consequence was to poison the well of education in a way that would cripple the society for decades to come.

Resistance to the Europeans had always, of course, been profound. After the military opposition of the previous centuries, there was, in 1889, for example, record of vehement political opposition by African leaders to the introduction of new pass laws. Four years later there occurred what seemed at the time to be a very small incident, but which was to have consequences that would reverberate around the globe. On a cold winter's night in 1893 a young British-trained lawyer, recently arrived from India, was travelling by train to Pretoria to deal with a case. His firm in Durban had bought him a first-class ticket, but when a white passenger got onto the train in Pietermaritzburg at 9 p.m. the lawyer was told to move to the van as he was patently 'coloured'. The young lawyer refused. He was pushed off the train and his luggage dumped beside him. He spent the night shivering in the waiting room, debating with himself whether or not he should simply return home to India. He decided that it was his duty to try to root out 'the deep disease of colour prejudice … and suffer hardships in the process'. He took the next train to Pretoria and so began the political trial by fire of Mohandas Gandhi, then aged 23. The following year he founded the Natal Indian Congress, and then, in the first decade of the new century, he pioneered his satyagraha ('soul-force') strategy of non-violent resistance in Johannesburg, burning passes and leading marches in defiance of unjust laws. Gandhi was jailed many times before he left South Africa in 1914 – on which occasion he presented to General Smuts, his

Mohandas Gandhi arrived in South Africa in 1893, aged 23, as a lawyer. He stayed 21 years, during which time he led many campaigns against discriminatory legislation and forged the satyagraha ('soul force') strategy which he was to use so effectively in the struggle for Indian independence.

Clements Kadalie was one of the most remarkable of the long line of trade-union leaders who worked – against overwhelming odds – for the betterment of labour's working conditions during South Africa's industrial revolution. Born in Malawi and trained as a teacher, he emigrated to South Africa in search of a better life. Soon after arriving in Cape Town in 1918 he was pushed off a pavement by a policeman and assaulted. Like Gandhi's removal from his train compartment, this small event was to have huge consequences, for it led directly to his founding of the ICU, which during the 1920s gathered massive support throughout the country, particularly from rural farmworkers.

prosecutor (and chief political opponent), a pair of sandals that he had made for him whilst in jail. Smuts was to wear these for many years until, on the occasion of the Mahatma's 70th birthday, he returned them. The methods that Gandhi later used to huge effect in India were also used in many subsequent political protests in South Africa, not least by African women in the Orange Free State in 1913. Led by Charlotte Maxeke, their protests effectively delayed the imposition of pass laws on African women for 40 years. There was also a seminal satyagraha campaign by the Indian community immediately after the Second World War.

The founding, in 1912, of what was to become (in 1923) the ANC grew out of an earlier movement to oppose the racism embedded in the Act of Union and was aimed at opposing the pending legislation to prohibit black South Africans from owning land. In the years after the First World War, however, the strongest black political force in the country was undoubtedly the Industrial & Commercial Workers Union (ICU), founded and led by the charismatic Clements Kadalie. He was an immigrant from Malawi and was particularly successful in ensuring that rural workers were part of the movement. The ICU grew exponentially during the 1920s, but in the end it was unable to sustain its success and gradually faded away in the mid-1930s. The ANC grew strongly, particularly after the Defiance Campaign in 1952 when over 8 000 people were arrested around the country for entering 'Europeans Only' sections of post offices and railway

stations, burning passes and generally disobeying racist laws. The government responded with legislation
that included flogging as a punishment for incite-
ment to such defiance. Subsequently the ANC, led by
Nkosi Albert Luthuli, Prof. Z K Matthews and others,
spearheaded a movement, involving a wide range of
extra-parliamentary opposition organisations, to adopt
a Freedom Charter (1955), which spelt out what were
to become the goals of a post-apartheid South Africa.
The government responded by charging 156 opponents of apartheid, including Luthuli, Matthews and
Nelson Mandela, with treason. In the end everybody
was acquitted, but the Treason Trial was to entangle
those accused for a long time.

Nkosi Albert Luthuli, president of
the ANC from 1952 to 1967.

Prof. Z K Matthews, first graduate
of Fort Hare, proposed the drawing
up of the Freedom Charter .

Five years later came another campaign against
the pass laws. In March 1960, in response to a call
by Robert Sobukwe of the Pan-Africanist Congress
(PAC), people marched peacefully to hand in their
passes at the police station in Sharpeville, south of
Johannesburg. The police opened fire and 69 people
were killed, many of them shot in the back as they
fled. The event sparked international outrage and led
to further peaceful marches in a tense South Africa.
The government response was to jail Sobukwe and to
ban both the PAC and the ANC. The reluctant move to
armed resistance by both Congress parties followed
almost immediately.

Other important streams of opposition included the
Natal (and later Transvaal) Indian Congress and the
Non-European Unity Movement, led by Dr Abdullah

Grievances against pass laws, low wages, shack removals and liquor raids were acutely felt as the policies of apartheid bit more deeply during the 1950s. In June 1959 police beat African women in Cato Manor, Durban (pictured). The women were protesting against state measures to close free-enterprise liquor outlets. Some months later there were widespread peaceful protests against the pass laws, but on 21 March 69 people were shot dead when a crowd gathered south of Johannesburg at the Sharpeville police station to hand in their passes.

Abdurahman. Abdurahman also helped found the Teachers' League of South Africa, which was to play a powerful role in battling for proper education, particularly in those schools in the Western Cape which were run by the Coloured Affairs Department. There was also the All Africa Convention, brought together under the leadership of Prof. DDT Jabavu. These organisations presented a united front of opposition to the legislation of 1936, which included a measure to remove the remnant of black voters in the Cape Province from the common voters roll. The PAC, led by Robert Sobukwe, broke away from the ANC at the end of the 1950s. Ten years later, the Black Consciousness movement began to make its presence felt on university campuses, filling the void left by the banning of the ANC and the PAC. In 1983 the United Democratic Front (UDF) was to emerge, almost overnight, at a volatile moment in the country's history, as a key provider of leadership for resistance to government-without-representation. The trade union movement too, particularly after it began to rebuild after textile strikes in December 1972, was to play a major role. The founding of the inclusive Congress of South African Trade Unions (Cosatu) in 1985 was the culmination of over 100 years of intense struggle by black workers for economic justice. All of these organisations, at different times and in different ways, fought at great cost – enduring banning, imprisonment, torture, exile and death – for the vision of a just and democratic society.

Robert Sobukwe, founder and president of the PAC, issued the call for people to hand in their passes on 21 March 1960. It was at one of these marches, to the police station at Sharpeville, that the police panicked, fired on a peaceful, unarmed crowd, and shot dead 69 people, many of them in the back.

Walter Sisulu burns his pass. Beloved mentor of the liberation movement, Walter Sisulu spent 26 years in prison, where he was the wise confidant not only of Nelson Mandela but of a whole range of political prisoners, not all of whom were members of the ANC.

Member of parliament from 1953 to 1989, Helen Suzman was for many of these years the sole voice of trenchant opposition to the laws and practices of the apartheid politicians.

APARTHEID: WHY?

It is only in countries where we find two races of different colours and where there is no legislation to bring about apartheid that the European eventually disappears. We have examples of it. There was no apartheid in Egypt; and what were the consequences? The British had to leave Egypt.

HT van G Bekker (NP)
House of Assembly, 1953

The Nationalist Government's policy is separate development. Now if a white man marries a black Transkeian woman, the man will be voting for the white parliament, the black for the Transkei parliament and the children for the Coloured Persons' Representative Council. I do not think this makes for a happy family life.

FW de Klerk explaining, in 1975, why
the Mixed Marriages Act was necessary

Ben Maclennan, Apartheid: The Lighter Side,
Chameleon Press, Cape Town, 1990

There were whites, too, who battled. A few people, like Helen Suzman of the Progressive Federal Party, used the protection of the whites-only parliament to fight for basic values. 'How often,' she once asked, when members of the official opposition had failed to oppose indefinite detention without trial, 'have I sat in Parliament and watched a shiver go up and down those green benches looking for a spine to crawl up?' Outside parliament, a small but intrepid band of women adopted for many years the technique of a silent vigil, whilst wearing a black sash, to demonstrate publicly against government attacks on the rule of law.

In the SACP, which contained both black and white members, many were banned, driven into exile or – like the famous advocate Bram Fischer – jailed. So too the Liberal Party, led by Alan Paton, whilst refusing to

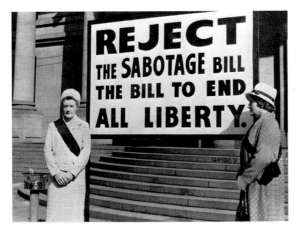

Over a period of 30 years, women of the Black Sash stood in silent protest to draw attention to racist and unconstitutional legislation. But they also ran advice offices to assist people – often women – caught in the coils of the pass and other laws.

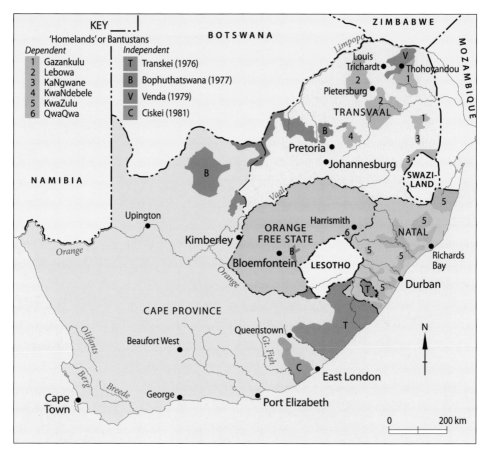

Apartheid South Africa. The Land Act of 1913 established the 'native reserves' outside of which black South Africans were not allowed to purchase land. These reserves became the core of the Bantustans, 'Homelands', and ultimately 'Black National States' (the four 'TBVC' states) of apartheid policy.

follow the path of armed resistance, had an inclusive membership and battled for the liberal values of a non-racial democracy. In the churches a number of individuals played prophetic roles – men like Trevor Huddlestone, who lived in Sophiatown where he played a major role in the struggle against forced removals and the introduction of Bantu Education in the 1950s; and Beyers Naude, who founded and led the Christian Institute until it was banned in 1977. So too did the imam Abdullah Haron, who died under suspicious circumstances in a police cell in 1969.

Of course, life was not all politics, although it is all too easy to overlook what people were doing in the fields of music and medicine, road-building and writing. Miriam Makeba mesmerised audiences of all colours with her singing, Abdullah Ibrahim played his jazz, Nadine Gordimer wrote her novels and Prof. Christiaan Barnard pioneered the world's first heart transplant in 1967 – to say nothing of boxing sensations like Jake Tuli, who won the British Empire flyweight title on his first fight outside South Africa, or Olympic gold medallists such as the swimmer Joan Harrison. These are but a few examples of the astonishing vitality that bubbled up everywhere, in spite of – or perhaps precisely because of – the tensions in society.

Miriam Makeba, one of the stars of Todd Matshikiza's musical *King Kong*, burst onto the national stage in 1959. She was forced to spend 30 years in exile, where she gained an international reputation. She returned to South Africa in 1990, where, as Mama Afrika, she continued both to sing and to encourage a new generation of singers.

9
A SOUTH AFRICAN MIRACLE?
1986-1996

To many people the change in South Africa from the aggres-
sive apartheid state of the mid-1980s to a democratic non-racial
society with one of the most progressive constitutions in the world
only ten years later seemed to be nothing short of a miracle. Yet,
for some of the more perceptive analysts, South Africa is a very
ordinary country where talk of miracles detracts from the need
for hard thinking about historical processes and future policy.
Looking back, it is possible to see a number of different forces
which together brought about the transition. What is clear is that
there was no single magic bullet to account for the sudden shift.
Rather a combination of factors helps to explain what happened.

The heavy-handed police crackdown on 16 June 1976 against schoolchildren
in Soweto – they were protesting against the new edict compelling them
to study mathematics and social studies in Afrikaans rather than English –
provoked a ten-year uprising of teenagers around the country. Here young
women confront the security forces in Langa, Cape Town.

The brightest, most charismatic and fearless leader of his generation, Steve Biko was battered unconscious by security policemen who then transported him naked, but manacled, from a police cell in Port Elizabeth to Pretoria, where he died on 12 September 1977 at the age of 30. His ideas, expressed most articulately in his book, *I Write What I Like* (1978), live on. Biko's influence was immense on the generation of students who took to the streets in the decade after the Soweto uprising of 1976.

IN THE YEARS AFTER THE SHARPEVILLE CRISIS OF 1960, many of the top resistance leaders were imprisoned, whilst others went into exile. After Robert Sobukwe of the PAC was sent to Robben Island for his role in the anti-pass campaign, Nelson Mandela, Walter Sisulu, Govan Mbeki and others in the ANC were tried in 1964 for plotting to overthrow the state. Freedom, said Mandela in his statement from the dock, is something 'for which I am prepared to die.' Contrary to the expectations of many, the men were not given the death sentence, but were jailed for life. In the years that followed, South Africa was a political desert. Racists ruled with an iron fist; any sign of black political opposition was ruthlessly crushed.

In this hostile climate the first inkling of change was new talk amongst black students about Black Consciousness. Whilst the authorities at first hoped that this indicated acceptance (at last) of the philosophy of apartheid, Steve Biko and others were developing ideas that were to renew and deepen black determination to be free. The degree to which events within South Africa during the 1970s were crucial to subsequent changes in the country has perhaps not been fully appreciated. But there seems little doubt that the Black Consciousness movement exerted a profound influence on the commitment of the younger generation to get rid of apartheid. 'It is better,' said Biko, 'to die for an idea that will live than to live for an idea that will die.' In June 1976, students from schools in Soweto, the huge black township on the south side of

Johannesburg, marched peacefully in protest at being taught in Afrikaans – in what had long been regarded as 'education for barbarism'. The police response of using guns and whips elicited furious protests, which spread like a forest fire through schools. Throughout the next decade, hundreds of young South Africans – of whom Biko was one – gave their lives in police cells, in prisons and on the streets of the country in the struggle for freedom.

The anger from below was one manifestation of another internal contradiction of the apartheid system. The policy of Bantu education, combined with the colour bar, was designed to keep blacks in low-skilled jobs at the bottom of the economic pyramid. But, as the economy grew, the demand for more highly skilled labour expanded faster than the supply of educated white workers. Thus there was increasing pressure from industry for a fundamental restructuring of education and training.

This period also saw a more concerted challenge to the pass laws. Matters came to a head in the mid-1970s in the city which the apartheid planners had chosen to be the whitest of all. In Cape Town, it had been decreed, the number of black South Africans would be reduced by 5% per year. But the need for labour continued to grow, women were determined to join their men, and self-built, illegal housing settlements grew. The state retaliated with every means at its disposal – including arrests, forced deportations, guns, dogs, bulldozers and arson – to demolish houses and force

Car workers and women in the retail industry were amongst those whose strikes began to change the balance of political power in South Africa after 1972.

Self-built housing along Modderdam Road was one of the main targets of the apartheid authorities in their attempt to prevent black families from settling in Cape Town during the 1970s.

the women back to the rural 'Homelands'. To no avail. They kept coming back because, as one of the women explained, 'ayiko mali': there was simply 'no money' in the areas to which they were being removed. Finally, after the destruction of many settlements, Crossroads (a community living in self-built housing near Cape Town airport) was granted a reprieve in 1979. It was a turning point. Pass law prosecutions in the first half of the 1970s had risen, under the pressures of urbanisation, to an average of some 540 000 cases each year – more than one person charged every minute, day and night. The system had become overloaded. In 1986 the pass laws were abolished. The apartheid vision of 'separate development', the moral fig leaf used to justify the policy, was in tatters. For if people were to live permanently in town, what value was separate citizenship in some rural 'Homeland'?

As early as 1977 Robert Sobukwe pointed out that the demands for communication within a modern industrial economy were such that the time would come when business leaders would be quietly urging government to recognise trade unions so that there could be reliable channels of communication through organisations that workers trusted. This was counter-intuitive at the time when the struggle for unionisation was at its height and hostility to worker power by both government and bosses was intense. But Sobukwe's analysis was correct. In 1979, black people were permitted to belong to registered trade unions for the first time. In 1980 there were 57 000 black members (7%)

In the four turbulent years after the 1990 release of political prisoners and the return of the exiles, 14 000 South Africans died in political violence. Church leaders were amongst those who believed that a 'third force' led by certain generals of the police and army was stoking conflict between black South Africans in order to derail talks and weaken the bargaining position of the ANC. Archbishop Desmond Tutu was amongst those who worked tirelessly – and with great courage – to defuse explosive situations. Here he is seen preaching to an angry crowd in Kagiso on the West Rand.

in the registered trade unions. By 1985 the number had risen tenfold to 511 000 (37%). The balance of power within the political economy had fundamentally altered.

Meanwhile the economy, which had grown fairly consistently down the years, was beginning to slow down precariously. The growth rate of GDP averaged 5.5% per year in the 1960s, fell to 3.3% in the 1970s, and in the 1980s was down to 1%, whilst the rate of job creation turned negative after 1986. With the decline of jobs in agriculture and mining, transformation of the economy needed a far greater proportion of skilled labour, and this required the sort of investment in human capital that was specifically discouraged by apartheid policy.

A combination of factors – the determination of rural women to move to town; the insistence of workers on the right to bargain for better working conditions;

and the courage of schoolchildren prepared to die for a better education – made for a new, highly volatile, political atmosphere within the country. To this explosive mixture was added, by PW Botha in 1983, a misguided attempt at constitutional reform by creating parliamentary representation (in separate chambers) for those classified 'Coloured' and 'Indian'. But apartheid's new constitution also made it clear that all those classified 'Bantu' belonged to their own ethnic 'Homelands' and were no longer to be citizens of South Africa. This was the last straw. The townships, under the leadership of the new UDF, with close links to the ANC-in-exile, became ungovernable: no-go areas for police and even the army.

Nor were these the only pressures. The collapse of the Portuguese empire in 1974 and the independence of Zimbabwe in 1980 removed the psychological protection of a white-ruled belt across the continent. The

International pressure – exerted by means of boycotts against all kinds of goods and activities, ranging from oranges and wine, through sport and business, to refusals to roll-over loans made from abroad – was increasingly felt not only by the businesses affected, but also by the apartheid government. Here a march in London protests the presence of the Springbok rugby players at Twickenham during their 1969–70 tour.

response of the South African government, with the implicit support of the CIA, was to send armed forces against the incoming Marxist-leaning government in Angola. The South African Defence Force was heavily involved in fighting, but overreached itself and eventually withdrew. The South African president found it increasingly difficult to explain to supporters why their sons, now returning in body bags, had been fighting beyond the borders when no war had been declared. South African involvement in Mozambique was less visible, but possibly even more destructive in its support of efforts by the conservative Mozambican National Resistance (Renamo) to destabilise Mozambique's new Frelimo government.

The real external threat to apartheid, however, came not so much from military forces led by Angolans, Cubans, or even by exiled South Africans in the form of Umkhonto we Sizwe ('Spear of the Nation', the

The Congress of South African Students (Cosas), which was founded after the state's heavy-handed repression of student protests in Soweto in 1976, was the main organising force behind the school boycotts that spread through the country during the following decade. Here students are marching to the funeral of a Cosas comrade in KwaMashu, Durban, in 1981.

President of the ANC during the 30 difficult years of exile (1960–1990), O R Tambo played a pivotal role in the South African revolution by holding the party together as a viable, broad-based and coherent movement which increasingly became seen in the outside world as a government-in-waiting.

military wing of the ANC), as in the form of economic sanctions. Ever since I B Tabata's pamphlet 'The boycott as a weapon for struggle', South Africans had been trying to use boycotts effectively. And not without success. The sports boycott, which systematically isolated South African rugby players, cricketers, Olympic athletes and others from the rest of the world, had a significant impact on white thinking. Fear of an international boycott of their wine had caused farmers in the western Cape to bring to an end in the 1970s the profitable system of farm jails in which farmers had shares, thus ensuring regular supplies of labour. But it was financial boycotts, spurred on by churches in Europe and North America, and by student pressures on American universities to withdraw their investments, that concentrated the minds of big business. When, in 1985, Chase Manhattan Bank in New York

As president, P W Botha was the first of the apartheid leaders to begin talking – ever so tentatively – with Nelson Mandela in July 1989. Botha subsequently lost power to FW de Klerk, who moved ahead more rapidly. But Botha was to meet Mandela again when the new president of a democratic South Africa visited him in his retirement.

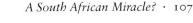

The first official meeting between the leaders of the ANC and the South African government took place at Groote Schuur in Cape Town in May 1990. Agreement was reached in a pact about political prisoners, exiles and security legislation.

refused to roll over important South African loans, the pressures started to mount. Big business within the country began to play a significant role in mediating between the apartheid government and the exiled ANC in Lusaka.

And then, quite unexpectedly, the Berlin Wall came down in 1989. For some analysts, this was a necessary and sufficient event for the ending of apartheid. It is true that once the Cold War ended the CIA no longer felt obliged to protect South African racists as opponents of Marxism. The white government felt more isolated than ever and also, so it claimed, was more willing to talk to a liberation movement that no longer had the might of the Soviet Union behind it. However, it would seem more accurate to describe the ending of the Cold War as something which facilitated the process of change in South Africa, but which did not cause it.

Emerging from the conservative wing of the ruling NP, FW de Klerk became president of South Africa in 1989 and rapidly displayed a pragmatic political dexterity which surprised everybody. In February 1990 he electrified the country and the world with his unexpected announcement to parliament that his government was ready to free all political prisoners, to unban all political parties and to permit all exiles to return home to participate in public life.

The negotiating skills of Cyril Ramaphosa – lawyer and former president of the National Union of Mineworkers – were such that the NP government ended up conceding far more power than it had originally envisaged.

For the government, Roelf Meyer led the long and tortuous negotiations which followed De Klerk's announcement.

Finally, there was the question of leadership. Most observers agree that, although President PW Botha had the first meeting with the prisoner Mandela, the change of leadership to FW de Klerk led to a more pragmatic and flexible approach, which Mandela was able to use in his strategy to negotiate freedom without strings attached. Both leaders, moreover, were able to persuade their followers to move to positions of compromise previously thought impossible. Talks about talks began in 1985 and continued until Mandela's release in February 1990. Mandela himself was careful to keep Oliver Tambo and the rest of the ANC leadership informed. Tambo's brilliant leadership had managed not only to hold a broad movement together in exile over nearly 30 years, but also, with the help of able younger leaders like Thabo Mbeki, had built diplomatic links around the world – so much so that when the time for negotiation came the ANC was able to present itself as the alternative government.

Thus, when all political prisoners were released and the previously banned political parties were allowed to operate freely, it was the ANC (in alliance with the SACP and Cosatu) which – despite Tambo's death in 1992 and the assassination of one of his ablest lieutenants, Chris Hani, a year later – took the lead in negotiations. Cyril Ramaphosa, who had honed his bargaining skills as the first general secretary of the National Union of Mineworkers, and Roelf Meyer of the NP worked out a settlement.

THE ELEVEN OFFICIAL HOME LANGUAGES
SPOKEN IN SOUTH AFRICA

According to the official census of 2001, the mother tongue of 45 million South Africans was made up as follows: isiZulu 24%; isiXhosa 18%; Afrikaans 13%; Sepedi 9%; English 8%; Sesotho 8%; siSwati 8%; Xitsonga 4%; Setswana 3%; isiNdebele 2%; Tshivenda 2%.

The first democratic elections were held on 27 April 1994 and the ANC won 63% of the votes, followed by the NP with 20%. The Inkatha Freedom Party, led by Prince Mangosuthu Buthelezi, got 11% of the votes and won the province of KwaZulu-Natal, whilst the conservative Freedom Front, led by General Constand Viljoen, and the more progressive Democratic Party each received 2%. The PAC, destroyed by exile, received only 1%. The three main parties formed a Government of National Unity, which lasted until the NP withdrew at the end of 1996. By this time the last step in the political transition had been taken with the adoption of the new Constitution in May 1996 and South Africa faced the world with the finest legal framework to protect human rights then in existence.

The political lightning and thunder that had played around South Africa during the months before the country's first ever democratic elections commenced on 27 April 1994, all died away as the day dawned and citizens joined the long queues to vote for their new government.

SOUTH AFRICA TODAY

Current problems facing the country – and there are many – cannot hide the astonishing achievements of the founding years of the newly democratic South Africa. This chapter considers what would appear, at this stage, to be the country's seven most significant achievements and then looks squarely at the seven greatest difficulties facing the country as it peers into the future. Many of these challenges have deep roots in the country's history, but must be overcome if South Africa is to fulfil its great potential. It is perhaps helpful to see South Africa as having indeed come a long way on the long walk to freedom, but the problems which remain are very serious and their solution will require no less commitment than did the long struggle to overcome colonialism and apartheid.

Yes we can! In winning the fiercely competitive race to host the biggest sporting event in the world, the FIFA World Cup in 2010, South Africa was able to point to its success in hosting other major events, including the Rugby World Cup in 1994 (which it won) and the Cricket World Cup in 2003.

Thabo Mbeki, who was effectively prime minister during the Mandela presidency and was himself, subsequently, twice elected president, wielded enormous power in South Africa from 1994 until 2008, when he was ousted by his own party.

IN THE TRANSITION FROM APARTHEID TO DEMOCracy, great negotiating skill (and not a little luck) prevented a downward spiral of violence into what many feared would become a bloodbath. Mandela himself was worried throughout the negotiation period after his release about a potential white uprising. There was also conflict – particularly in KwaZulu-Natal and on the Witwatersrand – which had the potential of erupting into a different kind of civil war. Exacerbated by vicious, shadowy 'third-force' attempts apparently backed by the state to promote intra-black violence, an explosive atmosphere was defused in a remarkable process of peace-making by leaders, including Jacob Zuma, within both the ANC and Inkatha.

South Africa's Constitution, in place since 1996, has been acclaimed as one of the world's finest. Understanding that human rights meant little to people trapped in poverty, the drafters of the Constitution included 'second generation' rights of citizens to basic needs, including housing. There has been widespread acceptance of Constitutional Court judgements throughout the process of dismantling the legal structure that entrenched racism.

When apartheid began, 33 people were executed annually. In the mid-1980s the average was 135. The new government moved immediately to abolish the death penalty and – despite being engulfed by a tidal wave of crime, and despite pressure from grass roots – the ANC government has stood firm, arguing that reintroducing it would be unconstitutional. The public process of the Truth and Reconciliation Commission (TRC), in which those who had tortured and murdered (for 'political reasons') were promised amnesty in return for telling the full truth, was controversial. Some felt that certain crimes deserved Nuremberg trials. Others maintained that the TRC should have concentrated only on apartheid protagonists and not also considered human rights abuses in the ANC exile camps. It was also argued that deeper horrors were ignored, such as the consequences of the single-sex migratory labour system. Be that as it may, the TRC was an astonishing achievement. For the first time in history, a country examined itself soon after it had committed wide-ranging violations of human rights. Moreover, the process, as led by Archbishop Desmond Tutu, elicited information that would never otherwise have been brought to light.

A temptation to which weak governments can succumb is macro-economic populism, whereby, in response to pressure for more public expenditure, the state uses deficit financing to spend far more than its tax revenue warrants. Inflation can then spin out of control, with harsh effects on pensioners and the poor; and with destabilising political consequences, as happened in Germany in the 1920s, Latin America in the 1970s and Zimbabwe under Robert Mugabe. In South Africa, disciplined management of the macro-economy by the country's first three democratic administrations was a significant achievement. Over the ten years between 1998 and 2007 the annual rate of infla-

A former member of the Security Branch, sitting on the back of a person whom he had tortured, demonstrates to the TRC how he used a cloth bag which would have been 'submerged in water to get it completely wet' to cut off the air supply, thus forcing the detainee to provide information. After beating and the use of electric shocks, suffocation was the third most common form of torture used by the South African security forces between 1960 and 1994.

tion averaged little more than 6%. Having inherited a bankrupt economy in which per-capita growth was negative and people were getting poorer, the new democratic government achieved a positive growth rate of gross domestic product, averaging 3.2% for the 13 years from 1995.

There has been a significant increase in social-security benefits. Pensions were raised and a child grant was introduced. The number of beneficiaries of social-welfare grants more than quadrupled from 2.6 million in 1993 to 11.9 million in 2007 (of whom 7.9 million were children). In addition, electricity and water provision were extended, particularly in rural areas. In only five years, from 1996 to 2001, the proportion of homes using electricity for lighting increased from 58% to 70%.

Turning now to the shadow side of the new South Africa, there are seven major problems. One of the most intractable difficulties inherited by the Mandela

Unemployment: young men with nothing to do, Taung, 1982.

THE 7 × 7 SOCIETY	
Significant Achievements	*Major Concerns*
Negotiated transfer of power	Widespread and rising unemployment
Defusing of potential civil war	Widespread poverty and deep inequality
Constitution enshrining human dignity, recognising 11 home languages and dismantling of racist legal structure	Lack of organisational capacity; weak local government
Abolition of capital punishment	Struggling education system
Truth & Reconciliation Commission	Corruption, crime and xenophobia
Disciplined macro-economic management	HIV/AIDS and tuberculosis
Major roll-out of social-security benefits	Environmental challenges

government was the level of unemployment. The national average of 30% in 1993 was as high as it had been in the United States at the time of the Great Depression 60 years before. But while for whites unemployment averaged only 5%, for black South Africans it was 39%. For black youth (under 25) two out of every three (65%) who wanted work could not find jobs. All this was due to the huge apartheid-driven differences in educational opportunities for blacks and whites, which meant that on the eve of the first democratic elections, when nearly two-thirds (61%) of white adult South Africans had matriculated at school, only one in nine (11%) black adults had done

Jacob Zuma became the country's 4th democratic president in May 2009 after peaceful elections in which the ANC won 66% of the vote. Its closest rival, the Democratic Alliance, won 17%.

The effective destruction of many of South Africa's great schools after the introduction of the Bantu Education Act in 1953 was a crippling blow. Healdtown, founded in 1855, where Nelson Mandela, Robert Sobukwe and many other leaders were educated, is now part of the Historic Schools Restoration Project.

Woman in her single-room mud house, 1984.

so. By 2000 unemployment had risen to 36% and by 2004 it was 41%.

Poverty remains widespread. By the end of Thabo Mbeki's presidency (1999–2008), approximately 50% of the population had monthly incomes too low to sustain a decent life. 'For me,' said Mrs Witbooi from a small town in the Karoo,

> poverty is not knowing where your next meal is going to come from, and always wondering when the council is going to put your furniture out, and always praying that your husband must not lose his job. To me that is poverty.

The continued uncertainty faced by those living in poverty, including woefully inadequate housing in towns and scarce water supplies in many rural areas, make a mockery of the expectations of those who voted with such hope in 1994. Poverty is combined with deep inequality. Of countries for which data is available, South Africa remains one of the two or three most unequal. Between 1994 and 2004, the salary of the average CEO of an intermediate to large company in South Africa rose from 37 times to 48 times that paid to a worker on the minimum wage. Having successfully begun the slow process of bridging racial divides in society, are South Africans going to be able to overcome the barriers of class?

The brilliance of the political leadership in managing the transition and the general competence of many members of the new cabinet masked, for a while, the weakness of the government's organisational capacity, but in many parts of the country municipal councils, hospital administrators and school principals are simply not up to the job of ensuring that the basic functions of their organisations are properly fulfilled. The net result has been a sad decline in the health and educational facilities available to those without the resources to pay for private services.

The willingness of young schoolchildren to go out into the streets, prepared to die for a better education, was one of the most remarkable facts of life in South Africa during the 15 years after the Soweto language protests in June 1976. When he returned home in 1991, O R Tambo was asked if he had a special message for the youth of South Africa. Yes, he said: 'Education, education, education.' And Mandela was saying the same thing. Yet ten years after democratic government took over, it was estimated that 80% of old Bantu-education state schools were not functional. Thus, only 2% of black school-leavers obtained at least 60% in their final matriculation examination compared to 35% of white children. The divide is even starker in terms of mathematics or science results. The failure of the educational system to prepare the next generation for jobs in the 21st-century economy contains the seeds of a major social and political catastrophe.

Violent crime has long been endemic to South Africa. In the rural resettlement camps of KwaZulu-Natal in the early 1980s, women described graphically their fear

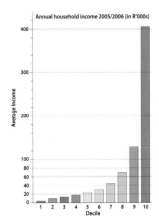

South Africa has one of the deepest levels of inequality in the world. Interpreting this graph, we see that the poorest 40% of households (deciles 1–4) had average incomes of less than R20 000 per annum whilst the richest 10% received over R400 000 per household. This was more than 90 times greater than the income of the poorest 10%.

while lying in bed alone in their homes as tsotsis (gangsters) roamed outside, ready to break in. Meanwhile in Cape Town the murder rate per million inhabitants was nearly three times higher than that of New York. Apartheid's forced removals, combined with the migrant labour system have wrought havoc on the social stability of earlier times. During the unsettled period of the transition, the number of murders more than doubled from 10 600 in 1988 to 24 900 in 1998 (but came down to 18 500 in 2007–8). Widespread rape,

Political satire has a long and honourable record in South Africa. Zapiro, the best cartoonist of his generation here makes fun of tensions within the tripartite governing alliance between the ANC, the SACP and Cosatu.

including that of babies and not excluding elderly grandmothers, was no less appalling a manifestation of the extent to which the social fabric of society had been torn apart by its recent history. This internal violence took a particularly nasty turn in 2008, when latent hostility to the presence of Africans from elsewhere on the continent suddenly erupted in widespread xenophobic attacks, particularly in poorer parts of urban areas, where competition for jobs is acute.

In addition to violent crime, there has also been widespread corruption. The demands of bureaucrats using their brief authority to extort money from citizens (and non-citizens), have been overshadowed by corruption on a far greater scale. Not all South African politicians have been immune to the destabilising temptations and corrupt pressures of the global military–industrial complex determined to sell arms.

Xenophobia.

Few people saw it coming. Before 1992 the proportion of pregnant women attending ante-natal clinics in South Africa who tested positive for the Human Immunodeficiency Virus was under 2%; by 2000 the proportion was 25%. Yet still the government, led by President Thabo Mbeki, was strangely blind to the harsh reality of this holocaust and its causes even though, by then, perhaps half a million South Africans had died due – directly or indirectly – to AIDS. Before the arrival of anti-retroviral drugs (whose dissemination was unnecessarily delayed in most parts of the country), it was estimated that by 2010 life expectancy would have fallen from its pre-epidemic high of 65 to 41 years, and that by 2015 the total number of people who would have died from AIDS-related illnesses might prove to be as high as 9 million. Even after a fundamental shift in medical policy brought about by grass-roots pressure from an active civil society, the plague continues to cut a wide swathe through South Africa.

Jan Smuts, twice prime minister of South Africa, is reputed to have said that even more important than the country's racial problems was the haemorrhaging of its topsoil through overgrazing. Not everybody would have agreed with him – if indeed he actually said it – but there is no doubt that environmental issues loom large in the country's future. Soil erosion; pollution of water sources; emission of greenhouse gases into the atmosphere by coal-fired power stations (together with the mining of labour through the migrant system): all point to a development process that has been essentially extractive in its philosophy. The social and external costs of production have seldom been considered, let alone measured. But consciousness of the fragility of the Spaceship Earth in which we all live requires fundamental rethinking about creating a sustainable political economy in the long term.

Looking back over South Africa's history and all that has been overcome – conquest, slavery, enforced migrant labour, legalised racism and tyrannical government – it is clear that the country has a great deal to be proud of in its struggle for freedom. But the problems that remain are no less daunting than those already overcome. A long walk still lies ahead, yet there is no

Soil erosion has been one of South Africa's major environmental concerns for a century and more. Here stone walls have been built in an effort to halt the destruction.

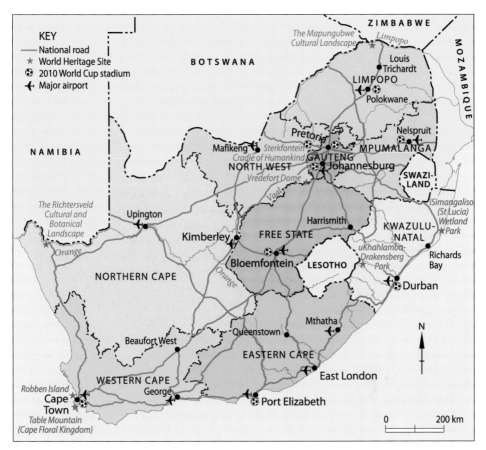

KEY
— National road
★ World Heritage Site
⚽ 2010 World Cup stadium
✈ Major airport

ZIMBABWE

The Mapungubwe
Cultural Landscape   Limpopo

BOTSWANA

Louis
Trichardt

LIMPOPO

Polokwane

MOZAMBIQUE

Pretoria

Nelspruit

NAMIBIA

Mafikeng   Sterkfontein
Cradle of Humankind   GAUTENG   MPUMALANGA

NORTH WEST   Johannesburg

Vredefort Dome   SWAZI-
LAND

Vaal

The Richtersveld
Cultural and
Botanical
Landscape   Upington

iSimangaliso
(St Lucia)
Wetland
Park

Orange

Kimberley   FREE STATE   Harrismith   KWAZULU-
NATAL

uKhahlamba-
Drakensberg
Park   Richards
Bay

Bloemfontein   LESOTHO

Orange   Durban

NORTHERN CAPE

Mthatha

N

Beaufort West   Queenstown

EASTERN CAPE

WESTERN CAPE   East London

George

Robben Island   Cape
Town   Port Elizabeth

Table Mountain
(Cape Floral Kingdom)

0   200 km

South Africa in 2010.

reason to suppose that a people who have achieved so much in the past cannot find within themselves the same courage and commitment that will be necessary in the future.

NOBEL PRIZE LAUREATES

Starting with Max Theiler in 1951 for his work in combating yellow fever, there have been ten South African-born Nobel Prize winners: Albert Luthuli (Peace, 1960); Allan M Cormack (Medicine, 1979); Aaron Klug (Chemistry, 1982); Nadine Gordimer (Literature, 1991); Desmond Tutu (Peace, 1984); FW de Klerk and Nelson Mandela (Peace, 1993); Sydney Brenner (Physiology or Medicine, 2002); J M Coetzee (Literature, 2003).

INDEX

PHOTO CREDITS

ACKNOWLEDGEMENTS

Many colleagues, friends and members of my family had to put up with a lot during the course of this book being written. Apart from much needed moral support they read, checked, corrected, edited and greatly improved earlier versions. Most of them read the whole typescript, some of them more than once. I am hugely grateful for all that they did and hope that they find the finished version to be worth all their efforts. Needless to say, I take full responsibility for any errors that may remain.

In particular I wish to thank:

Neville Alexander, Elisabeth Anderson, Adrian Arnott, Tanya Simons Barben, Geoffrey Budlender, Caroline Bundy, Maarten de Wit, Simon Hall, Adam Hochschild, Dudley Horner, Bill Nasson, John Parkington, Marguerite Poland, Mamphela Ramphele, Bruce Rubidge, Christopher Saunders, Martin West, Stephen Watson, David Wilson, Jessica Wilson, Lindy Wilson, Tanya Wilson, and three students from the Princeton Policy Task Force in Cape Town 2009 whose critiques remain anonymous.

Maps and illustrations are integral to the book and I am no less grateful for all the expert help I have received: to John Hall for drawing six specially commissioned maps; to Tanya Simons Barben (Rare Books and Special Collections, UCT), Fourie Botha (Umuzi), Carmen Hartzenberg (Struik), and Graham Goddard

(Mayibuye, UWC) for finding illustrations; and to Alison Siljeur and Lynn Woolfrey (Data First, UCT) who scanned everything to create the digital images needed. Librarians in the African Studies Library of the UCT Libraries were unfailingly supportive and efficient in helping to find books long out of print.

Special thanks to artists Lance Penny, Luis Rey, Jonathan Shapiro and Leigh Voigt for permission to use their sketches, paintings and cartoons; to Stephen Watson for his version of the /xam poem; and to twelve photographers who allowed me to reproduce their work: Paul Alberts, Omar Badsha, Amanda Ester-huysen, David Goldblatt, Benny Gool, Louise Gubb, John Hone, Carlo Kaminski, Ben Maclennan, Neil Rusch, Pippa Skotnes and Paul Weinberg.

And, of course, my publishers without whom …

Annari van der Merwe who accepted the idea before there was even a word on paper and then edited, with a vigorous pen, the writing which followed; Fourie Botha who has shaped and nursed the book as it all came together in the weeks before printing; Janice Evans who conceived the basic design; William Dicey who edited the final manuscript, planned the layout and set the text; Marius Roux who designed the cover; and Frederik de Jager and Stephen Johnson whose crucial support never wavered.